T0286880

Cambridge Elements ≡

Elements in Shakespeare Performance
edited by
W. B. Worthen
Barnard College

SHAKESPEARE AND NONHUMAN INTELLIGENCE

Heather Warren-Crow
Texas Tech University

CAMBRIDGE
UNIVERSITY PRESS

CAMBRIDGE
UNIVERSITY PRESS

Shaftesbury Road, Cambridge CB2 8EA, United Kingdom

One Liberty Plaza, 20th Floor, New York, NY 10006, USA

477 Williamstown Road, Port Melbourne, VIC 3207, Australia

314–321, 3rd Floor, Plot 3, Splendor Forum, Jasola District Centre,
New Delhi – 110025, India

103 Penang Road, #05-06/07, Visioncrest Commercial, Singapore 238467

Cambridge University Press is part of Cambridge University Press & Assessment,
a department of the University of Cambridge.

We share the University's mission to contribute to society through the pursuit of
education, learning and research at the highest international levels of excellence.

www.cambridge.org
Information on this title: www.cambridge.org/9781009202640

DOI: 10.1017/9781009202633

When citing this work, please include a reference to the DOI 10.1017/9781009202633

First published 2024

A catalogue record for this publication is available from the British Library.

ISBN 978-1-009-20264-0 Paperback
ISSN 2516-0117 (online)
ISSN 2516-0109 (print)

Shakespeare and Nonhuman Intelligence

Elements in Shakespeare Performance

DOI: 10.1017/9781009202633
First published online: April 2024

Heather Warren-Crow
Texas Tech University

Author for correspondence: Heather Warren-Crow, heather.warren-crow@ttu.edu

ABSTRACT: The Infinite Monkey Theorem is an idea frequently encountered in mass market science books, discourse on Intelligent Design, and debates on the merits of writing produced by chatbots. According to the Theorem, an infinite number of typing monkeys will eventually generate the works of Shakespeare. *Shakespeare and Nonhuman Intelligence* is a metaphysical analysis of the Bard's function in the Theorem in various contexts over the past century. Beginning with early-twentieth century astrophysics and ending with twenty-first century AI, it traces the emergence of Shakespeare as the embattled figure of writing in the age of machine learning, bioinformatics, and other alleged crimes against the human organism. In an argument that pays close attention to computer programs that instantiate the Theorem, including one by biologist Richard Dawkins, and to references in publications on Intelligent Design, it contends that Shakespeare performs as an interface between the human and our Others: animal, god, machine.

This Element also has a video abstract: www.Cambridge.org/Warren-Crow

KEYWORDS: William Shakespeare, artificial intelligence, Richard Dawkins, DNA, Intelligent Design

ISBNs: 9781009202640 (PB), 9781009202633 (OC)
ISSNs: 2516-0117 (online), 2516-0109 (print)

Contents

1 Three Propositions on the [   ] between Shakespeare and Monkeys

1.1 Juicy Mathematical Horror-Comedy in the Time of Performing Primates

Computer Says Monkeys Couldn't Write 'Hamlet' At Least Not So Far
Boyce Rensberger (1979)

Typewriting chimpanzees are surely extremely primitive artificial intelligences. They are rare, expensive, and slow.
            Vilém Flusser (*Into the Universe of Technical Images*, 2011: 25)

In 1979, Apple released the application "Infinite Number of Monkeys" on cassette tape as a standard part of the Apple II Computer System. Designed to demonstrate some of the capabilities of Integer BASIC and accompanied by code consumers could repurpose for their own needs, "Infinite Number of Monkeys" features a narrative that unfolds letter by letter on the screen. The story begins with the following: "It has been theorized for many years that if one were to set an infinite number of monkeys before an infinite number of typewriters they would eventually write all the great books of the world."[1] We soon learn that a scientist has installed 23,487 monkeys in a nineteenth century building once used for research on probability theory. "[A] finite number to be sure," the narrator admits, "but clearly enough to test the validity of the hypothesis . . . ." After a resonant description of the groaning of the decrepit building, we encounter the output of one of the simian test subjects. The following text is attended by "typewriter-like sound and hesitation" (accomplished computationally through a reusable subroutine created by the game's developer, Bruce Tognazzini): "MEVSGP MPIZ JBKQSI DBAPH TLUM XFEA HRBH CNUDNT PZIZDK VZOPZW DX. TO BE OR NOT TO BE THAT IS THE GZINCLE FORTEN GLAFFLE." Play the game again, and we may encounter the words of a bewilderingly tongue-tied Juliet:

---

[1] A screen capture of game play is available at www.youtube.com/watch?v=IfMDWhc_ohU.

"ROMEO, ROMEO, WHEREFORE ART THOU ROMEO. I'M DOWN IN THE PERFERFLAGENPYGA TLE RATTENFLOGER."[2] A garbled "Friends, Romans, Countrymen" is the third possible ending.[3] "So close . . . .so very close . . . .Perhaps with just a few more monkeys," the narrator sighs. Each pass has one of these three outcomes.

It is not a surprise that a failed Shakespeare is the punchline. "Infinite Number of Monkeys" references what is now called the Infinite Monkey Theorem, an idea well known in popular culture and the history of science. While these laboring monkeys might possibly write "all the great books of the world" – or, as astrophysicist Arthur Eddington puts it in 1928, "all the books in the British Museum," a translocation of mathematician Émile Borel's earlier suggestion of the French "Bibliothèque nationale" – the Anglophone cultural imagination most frequently charges them with the duty of reproducing Shakespeare's oeuvre (Borel, 1914/1920: 164; Eddington, 1928: 72).[4] What was once an absurd image of monkeys recreating an assorted collection becomes an equally absurd image of monkeys writing Shakespeare's complete works, just a sonnet, or, more often than not, *Hamlet* (as in the 2022 series *The Hamlet Factory*, a cartoon about an unending workplace of simian employees failing to hammer out the Bard's play). Sometimes, Shakespeare is retroactively inserted into early articulations of the Theorem, as he is in the article "Patents in an Era of Infinite Monkeys and Artificial Intelligence," which replaces the Bibliothèque nationale with the complete works of Shakespeare in a reference to Borel (Hattenbach and Glucoft, 2015: 33).

---

[2] This is from an unpublished, unpaginated manuscript generously shared with me by Bruce Tognazzini on August 22, 2022. Tognazzini wrote Infinite Number of Monkeys to teach himself how to program. "I then turned it into a platform for teaching others," he explains in an email sent to me on the same date. Tognazzini has had a long and impressive career as a software engineer, interface designer, and Human-Computer Interactions consultant.

[3] See above.

[4] The originator of the Infinite Monkey Theorem is likely Borel in his article "Mécanique Statistique et Irréversibilité" (1913) and subsequent book *Le Hasard* (1914), in which the "miracle des singes dactylographes" has a million monkeys trying to recreate the holdings of the "Bibliothèque nationale" and, elsewhere in the volume, all the books "dans les plus riches bibliothèques du monde" (1920: 164, 295).

While this is certainly a poor effort at researching citations, we might more generously conclude that "Shakespeare colonized the metaphor as it propagated through the 20th century," following Alan Galey in a broader argument regarding Shakespeare's "recruit[ment] to legitimate not only new technologies but also new ideas about the nature of information and data" (2014: 6). As if in support of Galey, Tognazzini's demo makes a joke about Shakespeare and monkeys and a nod to the pre-history of information science (i.e., nineteenth century probability theory) to promote the cutting-edge Apple II personal computer as a new kind of device capable of mainstreaming programming, then the purview of large institutions, corporations, and homebrew computer clubs.

The corporate vision of democratizing computation for profit would come true, of course. Seventeen years after Tognazzini's monkeys fail to produce, AI researcher Robert Wilensky reportedly takes a sporting jab at the AOL generation with the quip, "We've all heard that a million monkeys banging on a million typewriters will eventually reproduce the entire works of Shakespeare; now, thanks to the Internet, we know this is not true" (Radcliffe, 2016).[5] In 2007, Andrew Keen similarly likens Internet users to monkeys with the petulant claim that although the Infinite Monkey Theorem originally looked like a joke, it "now seems to foretell the consequences of a flattening of culture that is blurring the lines between traditional audience and author, creator and consumer, expert and amateur. This is no laughing matter" (2007: 2). Instead of "a masterpiece – a play by Shakespeare, a Platonic dialogue, or an economic treatise by Adam Smith," we have Google, which uses our inputs to assemble an aggregate stupidity passing as "collective intelligence" (Keen, 2007: 2, 6). There is nothing more horrifying than websites "making monkeys out of us without our even knowing it" (Keen, 2007: 6). While likening human beings to nonhuman primates has long been a white supremacist move, the late-twentieth

---

[5] This is frequently quoted, often using slightly different words, and sometimes identified as of dubious provenance. It is included in the online *Oxford Essential Quotations* at www.oxfordreference.com/display/10.1093/acref/9780191826719 .001.0001/q-oro-ed4-00011578;jsessionid=5E6BFE6BCECAD48128727 0B93F675961.

century would add other meanings to the image of the human monkey: the massified user of networked media, compelled by "monkeylike shamelessness," and, in the form of the code monkey, the low level, easily replaceable programmer, a geekier grease monkey (Keen, 2007: 3).

Large numbers of simian netizens would later LOL and turn meta with 2022's Infinite Monkey Theorem meme on TikTok. Many of the videos are like *The Hamlet Factory* in their empathetic concern for the monkeys as exploited laborers, stand-ins for the tech-necked web surfers of the post-industrial economy. The generic composition of the meme is a close-up of a user's face overlaid with self-consciously florid text. One example has a larf at the Shakespearean imperative by giving us what happens when the monkeys mistakenly recreate the works of Charles Dickens: a stunning accomplishment to be sure, but "The monkeys are disciplined."[6] A similar contribution has a monkey write *Macbeth* in binary code. "[C]orporate says that it is not valid."[7] When viewed collectively, this meme implicitly presents the mathematics of the Infinite Monkey Theorem as a kind of formal horror in which outcomes are either perfect or invalid, on or off, zero or one, and Shakespeare is exceptional not because of the quality of his writing, but because the set of {not Shakespeare} in an infinite universe is infinitely larger. By January of 2024, #infinitemonkeytheorem on TikTok had 10.3 million views.[8]

TikTokery from 2022, an animated series from the same year, patent law reviewed in 2015, a polemic from 2007, a text game from 1979, Integer BASIC released in 1976, an astrophysicist writing in 1928, a mathematician writing 14 years prior, and, yet to be met, competing chatbots, evolutionary biology, love letters in the sand, swallows, Harold Bloom, Alan Turing, Turing's chalk, alien communication, Darwinists, Betelgeuse, Paracelsus, gnomes, genii, urology, godhead, Mount Everest, St. John, Francis Bacon, Claude Lévi-Strauss, snow crystals, and incisor [   ] canine. Not to mention

---

[6] www.tiktok.com/@jackladuk/video/7076907403454729478?is_copy_url=1&is_from_webapp=v1.

[7] www.tiktok.com/@larz092/video/7079566586687868203?is_from_webapp=1&sender_device=pc&web_id=7120799983690925611.

[8] www.tiktok.com/tag/infinitemonkeytheorem.

Shakespeare, monkeys, typewriters, and, usually, infinity (although we have already seen versions that reach not for the infinite but just for the very large).

In short: *Shakespeare and Nonhuman Intelligence* is a metaphysical analysis of the Bard's performance in the Infinite Monkey Theorem as it has reemerged in varied contexts over the past century. I will not read Shakespeare's work for evidence of the nonhuman. Instead, I will read Shakespeare's function as a nonhuman writer, as a figure commonly understood to have written with nonhuman intelligence – or rather, non/human intelligence – and as ~~a figure~~ THE face of writing in the age of machine learning, bioinformatics, secularism, and other alleged crimes against the subject and the human organism most generally. With its writing technology, nonhuman primates, and, typically, infinity, the Infinite Monkey Theorem asks us to consider writing as an *anthrodecentric* endeavor even when it ultimately reinstates our investment in human and Shakespearean exceptionality. Instead of the death of the author, that old dream of Roland Barthes, the Infinite Monkey Theorem gives us the author's uneasy reanimation. As will later become clear, this reanimation operates at a distance, for the Bard is a necessary machinic component of a writing device that links monkeys and typewriters but keeps him outside of that circuit, off center, lurking in the outer margins like a god or Maxwell's demon.[9]

This lengthy introductory section will detail the following three propositions: (1) the Infinite Monkey Theorem is a philosophical toy, (2) the Infinite Monkey Theorem is an anthropogenic machine, and (3) the Infinite Monkey Theorem is a diagram of writing and its affiliation with the non/human – that is, with the technological, the animal, and the divine. All relevant definitions and the relationship between these three propositions and Shakespeare will be explained as the section proceeds.

Note: in determining the style of this volume, I decided to stage a loving confrontation between contradictory discourses, take Reddit both playfully

---

[9] Throughout this volume, I capitalize the word *God* if I am referring to the Christian God (of most direct relevance to the theories of Intelligent Design I address here) or retaining the capitalization when quoting another author. I leave the word in lower case if I am discussing a divine being more broadly conceived or indicating the applicability of many specific kinds of sacred, supernatural entities.

and seriously, include textual runs with defined parameters (mainly, the forms of the unnumbered and numbered list), and incorporate alphabetic nonsense as well as programming language and arcane genomic code. I tried to pitch my textual voice to the vibration of speculative thought appropriate to our age.

1.2 The Toy Anthropogenic Machine

The first reference to Shakespeare in the Infinite Monkey Theorem is from astrophysicist James Jeans's runaway hit *The Mysterious Universe* from 1930.[10] Drawing out the wondrous philosophical implications of quantum physics, cosmology, thermodynamics, statistical mechanics, and probability theory, Jeans marvels at the emergence of our sublime universe in a quotation worth recounting at length:

> It was, I think, Huxley who said that six monkeys, set to strum unintelligently on typewriters for millions of millions of years, would be bound in time to write all the books in the British Museum. If we examined the last page which a particular monkey had typed, and found that it had chanced, in its blind strumming, to type a Shakespeare sonnet, we should rightly regard the occurrence as a remarkable accident, but if we looked through all the millions of pages the monkeys had turned off in untold millions of years, we might be sure of finding a Shakespeare sonnet somewhere amongst them, the product of the blind play of chance. In the same way, millions of millions of stars wandering blindly through space for millions of millions of years are bound to meet with every kind of accident; a limited number are bound to meet with that special kind of accident which calls planetary systems into being. (1930/1938: 14–15)

[10] *The Mysterious Universe* sold 70,000 copies in the UK in its first year of print and led to a series of BBC radio lectures. Jeans's book was as infamous as it was famous, incurring criticism for its philosophical approach to physics (Helsing, 2020: 38, 41).

Actually, it was not Thomas Henry Huxley the Darwinist but Arthur Eddington the astrophysicist whose writing on monkey authorship Jeans likely read, and the relevant details from Eddington's *The Nature of the Physical World* include not a broad expanse of time to complete the task but a large number of laborers.

Jeans's faulty memory – or willful misattribution, as Eddington was his professional rival – alters the reference in other ways. Eddington's image of monkeys, machines, and archives is not one of exalted accident but of probability that is calculable but so unlikely as to be functionally impossible. "If I let my fingers wander idly over the keys of a typewriter it *might* happen that my screed made an intelligible sentence. If an army of monkeys were strumming on typewriters they *might* write all the books in the British Museum," Eddington writes. However, the exceptionally slim likelihood of such events leads to scientific certainty worthy of Law. He puts this "absurdly small" possibility in relation to the Second Law of Thermodynamics, which states that the entropy (disorganization or randomness) of a closed system increases over time. "The chance of [monkeys typing all the books in the British Museum] is decidedly more favourable" than the chance of molecules reorganizing themselves in one half of a vessel after being let out of a partitioned chamber and allowed to escape into the other half (1928: 72). While a complete return to their original home is one potential microstate, its possibility is, for our purposes, practically zero (for *on averag*e, a thermodynamic system becomes less organized as time proceeds). Not really gonna happen, but the faint possibility can be calculated. Evolutionary biologist Richard Dawkins explains a similar idea with "If you took all the cells of a swallow and put them together at random, the chance that the resulting object would fly is not, for everyday purposes, different from zero" (2015/ 1986: 14). While Jeans puts monkeys to work in order to make a case for the existence of marvelous, improbable things, assuming we give them enough time (for a sun to be found burning amidst Betelgeuses, to offer a Jeansian example, or for "If the dull substance of my flesh were thought" to be inscribed somewhere in the "vast meaningless distances" of the mostly unpopulated terrorverse), Eddington tasks those same monkeys with demonstrating the kind of certainty that arises from the knowledge that some things are so unlikely that scientists rightfully ignore them (Jeans, 1930/1938: 13).

Between Jeans's accidental sonnet and Tognazzini's corrupted *Hamlet* are references to monkeys typing Shakespeare's work in popular and academic texts on physics, molecular biology, information science, computer science, philosophy, and theology. The Infinite Monkey Theorem quickly emerges as a go-to reference in investigations of probability, meaning, agency, and/or intention. More to my point, as I argue throughout this volume, monkeys "unintelligently" and improbably tapping out Shakespeare's ever meaningful poetry are participants in longstanding discussions concerning the relationship between humans and our Others, such as machines, nonhuman animals, and divine beings. Given this history of the Theorem, it tracks that Dawkins would design a computer program to simulate monkeys typing *Hamlet* as part of an argument against creationism and what would later be called Intelligent Design (commonly shortened to ID). And yet, proponents of ID also use the Theorem to support their own central tenets. Shakespeare not only serves as the third point of what Dominic Pettman calls the "cybernetic triangle" – machine, animal, human – but as a back door for God to enter the discussion (ID) or be banished from the house (Dawkins) (Pettman, 2011: 5).

Dawkins's atheist computer simulation builds on the work of physicist William Ralph Bennett, Jr., who created a similar series of programs based on *Hamlet* in 1976, albeit with a different purpose. Bennett's experiments had multiple objectives: to model computational thinking for a wide range of undergraduates, show off the capabilities of BASIC, and investigate the statistical properties of literature. He discusses his process and findings in *Scientific and Engineering Problem-Solving with the Computer* (a textbook on programming in BASIC) and in "How Artificial Is Intelligence?," published in *American Scientist* the following year. The essay opens with the provocative tagline "The great works of literature and art are not merely rare statistical fluctuations, but are they simply the products of correlation matrices?," and then moves to a summary of the Infinite Monkey Theorem (1977: 694). "Nearly everyone knows that if enough monkeys were allowed to pound away at typewriters for enough time, all the great works of literature would result" (1977: 694). *Hamlet*, though, is Bennett's primary focus. While I will attend to Bennett's speculations on the nature of literary genius in the next section, I want to spend some time with these programs to lay out the computational thinking necessary for programming Shakespeare.

Bennett's exploratory reasoning unfolds by degrees, beginning with the invitation to imagine a typewriter with twenty-eight characters – all the capital letters of the English alphabet plus space and apostrophe. Examining Act III of *Hamlet*, Bennett's preferred test case, the physicist determines the distribution of these characters and decides that the imagined typewriter should have 6,934 space keys, 3,277 E keys, 2,578 O keys, and so on, with a total of 35,224 (1977: 695). A monkey's unintelligent clanging is purportedly the same as a random number being chosen between 1 and 35,224. Bennett calls this the first-order monkey problem and calculates the length of time for a monkey to type only the first two words of Hamlet's soliloquy: three days (1977: 695–696). Not good enough.

Bennett then gathers second- and third-order correlation data (fourth-order for the *American Scientist* article) from the same section of *Hamlet*. Second-order correlations indicate the frequency of two characters appearing together, with third-order correlations referring to the frequency of three-letter combinations. For the second-order monkey problem, Bennett asks us to consider the construction of twenty-eight typewriters and the directive to replace one typewriter with another as soon as a monkey strikes a key (1976: 117). The character typed would thus determine which of the other typewriters should be placed in front of a confused or delighted monkey, and the distribution of characters on the new typewriter (in other words, the way the dice are loaded) would be based on the likelihood of individual characters following the monkey's original pass. Bennett's computer simulation of this amusing scenario gives us the following:

> AROABLON MERMAMBECRYONSOUR T T ANED
> AVECE AMEREND TIN NF MEP HIN FOR'T
> SESILORK TITPOFELON HELIORSHIT MY ACT
> MOUND HARCISTHER K BOMAT Y HE VE SA FLD
> D E LI Y ER PU HE YS ARATUFO BLLD MOURO ...
> (1976: 119)

Each additional order increases the yield of recognizable words. He writes a program to solve the third-order monkey problem and returns with charming text, including "HAMLET OF TWE AS TO BE MURGAINS

FART ASSE GIVE ONEGS LOVE GODY BE HALLETURN ... "
(1976: 122). The *New York Times* summarizes Bennett's work in "Computer
Says Monkeys Couldn't Write 'Hamlet' At Least Not So Far" (Rensberger,
1979). Sure, Bennett does not successfully write a program to reproduce
Hamlet. The *New York Times* misses the point, but reaches a baser truth: the
cybernetic triangle, that "unholy trinity of human, animal, and machine,"
diagrams a condition of possibility in which failure may occur but success is
always not so far out in the future (Pettman, 2011: 5).

Perhaps anticipating the reality of legitimately offensive AI – take
Microsoft's teenaged Twitterbot, who turned into a "racist asshole in less
than a day" – Bennett is worried about the foul language of monkey typists
(Vincent, 2016). After repeating the second-order monkey program with
Edgar Allen Poe's "The Gold Bug," he gets the marvelous word
"FOLERESHIT" (an echo of "HELIORSHIT" from his Shakespeare
simulation), surmising that "the common four letter obscenities merely
represent the most probable sequences of letters used in normal words" in
the English language (1977: 699). Although the computational "preoccupa-
tion with vulgarity" is even more pathological in the third-order, he insists,
Bennett mysteriously assumes that "dirty-word strings" are more common
in low-order correlations (1976: 123). And with an uncharacteristically
classist claim, Bennet "notes the parallel in real life that the people who
use [expletives] the most also seem least educated," explicitly connecting
higher correlational orders, which are computationally dependent on
increased computing power, and perceived level of education (1976: 123).

While Bennett has little sense of humor when it comes to the gutter
mouths of his shameless monkeys, his general approach to recreating
Hamlet is one of intellectual play. Bennett demonstrates the value of such
lively computational thinking, both abstract and applied, to the study of
authorial voice in literature and, briefly proposed, music (1976: 128).[11]

---

[11] Here, Bennett is not suggesting something new, as the field of computational
stylistics was already established by the 1966 founding of the journal *Computers
and the Humanities* and publication of *The Computer and Literary Style*. That said,
computational research on literature in the 1960s and 1970s was dominated by the
creation of concordances, leaving stylistics relatively underdeveloped.

Seventeen years later, Stephen Clausing returns to Bennett's work as a prime early example of "speculative thought" within the then emerging discipline of humanities computing, later called digital humanities (1993: 249). Clausing's plea for more "humanistic speculation" resonates with one of Bennett's goals in writing his textbook on programming in BASIC: to use engaging and sometimes comic propositions to motivate college students from outside of the STEM fields to become programmers (Clausing, 1993: 249). The physicist includes a full-page portrait of Arthur Eddington with the face of a baboon, smiling, drawn in marker by Bennett's son, and a workbook problem to solve a cipher based on the First Quarto of *Hamlet*, introduced after a section on the history and practice of cryptography (1976: 125, 179, 155–158). Shakespeare performs a coupling function for Bennett the educator, securing the humanities to computer programming with the promise of ludic discovery.

Released the same year as the *New York Times* profile of Bennett's "Shakespearean gibberish," Tognazzini's text game for the Apple II starts with a sentence very similar to the beginning of Bennett's "How Artificial Is Intelligence?," connecting academic computer science to a gag to entertain and instruct the amateur programmer (Rensberger, 1979). Relevant here is an aside by Andrej Karpathy, maker of a Shakespeare generator created in 2015 through Recurrent Neural Networks: "their magical outputs still find ways of amusing me."[12]

On the topic of amusement, computers, and infinite fur: On April Fool's Day of 2000, the Internet Society published a jokey RFC (Request for Comments, a formal memorandum that distributes new research or proposes changes to Internet protocols) titled *The Infinite Monkey Protocol Suite* (IMPS).[13] According to the document's introduction, IMPS "is an experimental set of protocols that specifies how monkey transcripts may be collected, transferred, and reviewed for either historical accuracy (in the case of Shakespearean works) or innovation (in the case of new works). It also provides

---

[12] karpathy.github.io/2015/05/21/rnn-effectiveness/.

[13] Since 1989, Internet researchers from such bodies as the Internet Engineering Task Force, the Internet Architecture Board, and the Internet Society have released humorous RFCs as an April Fool's Day ritual.

a basic communications framework for performing normal monkey maintenance."[14] The document has a number of clever acronyms that demonstrate the lengths some will go for luulllzzzz: *ZOOs (Zone Operations Organizations) maintain the monkeys and their equipment, obtain transcripts from the monkeys' typewriters, and interact with other entities who evaluate the transcripts./A SIMIAN (Semi-Integrated, Monkey-Interfacing Anthropomorphic Node) is a device that is physically attached to the monkey. It provides the communications interface between a monkey and its ZOO. It is effectively a translator for the monkey. It sends status reports and resource requests to the ZOO using human language phrases, and responds to ZOO requests on behalf of the monkey./The BARD (Big Annex of Reference Documents) determines if a transcript matches one or more documents in its annex.*[15]

The Infinite Monkey Theorem is ridiculous and scientific, populist and professional, for experimentation and for laughs. That is – and here is my first proposition – **the Infinite Monkey Theorem follows the grand tradition of the nineteenth century philosophical toy.** The best-known examples of philosophical toys are devices used to illustrate aspects of the physiology of vision and/or the physics of light, both topics considered part of natural philosophy, a designation commonly in use until the twentieth century. These objects include the thaumatrope, a disk on a string that, when put in motion, creates an image superimposing the pictures on each of its two sides; and the stereoscope, a stand for two photographs positioned at a precise distance so our visual apparatus can combine the images into one apparently three-dimensional scene. Although the heyday of the philosophical toy was the Regency and Victorian eras, their spirit can be extended into the twentieth and twenty-first centuries. Take Sigmund Freud's use of the Mystic Writing Pad in 1924 to explain the operation of perception, consciousness, and memory; Alan Turing's refashioning of a party game for his groundbreaking 1950 article "Computer Machinery and Intelligence"; game theory's interest in poker and baseball as a "*metaphor*" for "serious interactions" like "market competition, arms races and environmental pollution" (qtd. in Franchi, 2005: 96); and the focus on recreational mathematics, chess, checkers, and go in computer

---

[14] www.ietf.org/rfc/rfc2795.txt.

[15] www.ietf.org/rfc/rfc2795.txt.

science. The concept of the philosophical toy as I define it is applicable to objects sold to the public as educational amusements, games appropriated for rhetorical purposes in academic scholarship or used as test cases in scientific research, and, most relevant here, entertaining intellectual constructions that affectively engage both STEM practitioners and enthusiasts.

Whether it emerges through written description or is concretized via computer programming, the Infinite Monkey Theorem is a machine for seeing, like the philosophical toy of the nineteenth century drawing room. In this case, what is seen is not the nature of human vision, as with the stereoscope, but the nature of the human, itself. In other words – and here is my second proposition, one that addresses the kind of philosophical toy we're playing with – **the Infinite Monkey Theorem is a toy anthropogenic machine**. A concept developed by Giorgio Agamben, the anthropogenic (also called anthropological) machine is a discursive assemblage that allows the human to be seen by showing what purportedly the human is not; that is, it is "an optical machine constructed of a series of mirrors in which man, looking at himself, sees his own image always already deformed in the features of an ape" (2004: 26–27). Agamben's close reading of the function of the machine reveals the contradictions of its deformational operation: it both does and does not distinguish between human and nonhuman animals, in the manner of disavowal (I know, but all the same). It vibrates most intensely at the "zone of indeterminacy" between ape and man, to which various Othered *Homo sapiens* – people of color, indigenous people, children, women, people with disabilities, the poor, for example – have been violently relegated (2004: 37). The nineteenth century obsession with the so-called missing link left some of the most committed scientists of the human with a frustrating aporia: the empty space (missing) between the human and the animal is also a connection between them (link). Even Carolus Linnaeus, eighteenth century refiner of the modern system of binomial nomenclature (which established the mise-en-scène for nineteenth century evolutionary science), notes wryly that while Linnaeus the Christian acknowledges that "Man is the animal the Creator found worthy of honoring with such a marvelous mind and which he wanted to adopt as His favorite," at the same time, Linnaeus the Naturalist sees just about no difference between humans and apes "save for the fact that the latter have an empty space between their canines and their other teeth" (qtd. in Agamben, 2004: 23–24). To bring us back to the twenty-first century: the queasy dystopian humor of much of #infinitemonkeytheorem plays with what Jean Feerick and Vin Nardizzi call, in the context of Renaissance literature, the "potential for human indistinction" (2012: 2). This is precisely what the anthropogenic machine, toy or otherwise, can inadvertently express through its fraught taxonomic routines.

Although Agamben's immediate motivating concern is the violence of dehumanization, his diagram of the anthropogenic machine has proven useful to the fields of animal studies and the broader environmental humanities, which have rightly argued that the exploitation of nature and the inextricability of humans and nonhumans are matters of social justice. Pettman's contribution to animal studies further expands upon Agamben's idea of "an abstract apparatus comprising all those potent symbols, figures, and tropes of belonging and exclusion" to account for the *material* technics of the machine's operation (Pettman, 2011: 7–8). Given the originary technicity of *Homo sapiens* – that is, the importance of tool use to the evolutionary development of our species – Pettman's re-technologization of Agamben's discursive machine is a key refinement, and one that is essential to my approach to Shakespeare and the Infinite Monkey Theorem.

Importantly, Pettman identifies Shakespeare as "without question one of the major engineers of the anthro-machine" (2011: 17). "[I]f Shakespeare did not exist," he continues, "we would have to invent him. For humanity requires an impressively ornate mirror in which to contemplate itself, to judge the effects of time, and to reassure itself of its enduring beauty" (2011: 18). Pettman's focus is less Shakespeare the author than the big dick energy of Harold Bloom, who insists that Shakespeare invented the human. Pettman undercuts this assertion with accusations of elitism and reminders of the colonialist underpinnings of "capital-C Culture" (2011: 18). While "Shakespeare had an immeasurable impact on our own identity and, by extension, our identity crises," he avers, "the question must surely be asked whose identity is at issue" (2011: 17). For Pettman and for me, the answer is most certainly Western, white, gendered as masculine, and although he doesn't mention it, able-bodied, I assume. Pettman uses an extended summary of Bloom's argument as an illustration of "the ideological cargo smuggled into the discussion inside the clenched cheeks of this key protagonist: the human" (2011: 13–14). The anthropogenic machine provides the clenching action that conceals and reveals its own most precious components.

Shakespeare could not function as such a widely admired, impressively ornate mirror if we didn't first secure his writings. More precisely, his role in the Infinite Monkey Theorem requires that his texts be separated from the complex material and social histories of what Alan Galey calls "the Shakespearean archive" – "the imagined totality of playbooks, documents, versions, individual variants, commentaries, sources, adaptations, and other preservable records that underwrite the transmission of Shakespeare's texts" (2014: 3). For *Hamlet* to be used as an appropriate standard to measure the success or failure of monkey/ Shakespeare simulations, the veritable "Tower of Babel" formed from the "accumulated mass of Shakespeare editions" must necessarily be obscured, and the "historicity" of "the ubiquitous public-domain Shakespeare text used by many digital projects," the nineteenth century Moby Shakespeare, must be strategically forgotten (Murphy, 2003: 4; Galey, 2014: 39). The long and oft-cited history of contesting Shakespeare's authorship may have driven crypta-nalytic innovation, the development of the field of computational stylistics, hundreds of years of popular speculation, and, perhaps, our weird obsession with Shakespeare bots, as I later discuss; however, outside of Shakespeare studies, the plays and sonnets themselves are usually treated as unique, unmediated scripture. Without these fixed elements, the monkey/typewriter assemblage would fall apart – or rather, its state of function could not even be known. Questions like "Which *Hamlet*?" necessarily have no place within the Infinite Monkey Theorem.

That said, the aim of *Shakespeare and Nonhuman Intelligence* is not to correct Infinite Monkey Theorists (or, for that matter, ID theists who claim to do information science or evolutionary scientists who don't understand *Hamlet* or chatbots misled by their dataset). The Infinite Monkey Theorem is a toy, and Theorists play fast and loose. Instead, my goal is to examine the toy, itself, to turn it around in my palm, to locate the Bard in this small anthropogenic machine, and to determine his operation. Paying particular attention to Dawkins's monkey/Shakespeare program, I consider the ways in which the figure of Shakespeare is performed as both an emissary of the human and an interface between human, animal, god, and machine. In this way, the Infinite Monkey Theorem is a rejoinder to Karen Raber's observation that Shakespeare, "whatever and whoever he was originally, has become a placeholder for all the things we want to believe make us [as humans] exceptional" (2018: 165). The Theorem is driven by Bardolotry, yes. *At the same time*, it asks us gamely to think, if only for a moment, that Shakespeare and the rest of his species might not be all that special. In other words, it both reinforces and destabilizes the uniqueness of Shakespeare and *Homo sapiens*, in the manner of the anthropogenic machine. With this in mind, we might understand the figure of Shakespeare in this context as less a place to be held than a mechanism of transduction in which the human may become especially human, a creature of nature, truly angelic, and/or an entertaining device.

Even when concretized in code or visualized as correlation matrices, the Infinite Monkey Theorem is really a thought experiment, one that allows the anthropogenic machine to operate quietly underneath more obvious considerations of randomness, infinity, creativity, and agency. The Theorem, it could also be said, does not necessarily care much about monkeys, hence its adoption as a philosophical toy by computer scientists transforming the image of simian labor into algorithmic iteration. Nonetheless, the Theorem *was* once literalized – and unambivalently concerned with monkeys – in a 2002 work of performance art involving a community of Sulawesi Crested Macaques (*Macaca nigra*) at the Paington Zoo Environmental Park in Devon in the UK. Part of a broader endeavor called the Vivaria Project, *Notes towards the Complete Works of Shakespeare* invokes the Infinite Monkey Theorem in order to challenge the idea that "monkeys producing actions" are the same as "a random generator such as a computer. On the contrary, it is possible that the monkeys will eventually produce the complete works of Shakespeare, but not simply because of chance. Also because they can think and learn."[16] The performance piece includes the installation in the macaque enclosure of a blue iMac and keyboard protected by acrylic cases, live updates on a website, a webcam that captures the monkeys' everyday activities and interactions with the keyboard, and a leather-bound publication with William

---

[16] The video "Notes Towards the Complete Works of Shakespeare," which explains the aims of the project, is available at vimeo.com/28979361.

Shakespeare's nearly illegible signature embossed in gold on the cover. The resulting document records the monkeys' extreme preference for the letter "S" (7,241 times in a row) and dislike of all vowels except for "A" (Elmo et al., 2002: unpaginated). "The joke, if indeed there is one," a video produced for the project explains, "must not be seen to be at the expense of the monkeys, but on the popular interest in the idea, especially those in the computer science and mathematics community interested in chance, randomness, autonomous systems, and artificial life."

The objective of *Notes towards the Complete Works of Shakespeare* is to draw attention to the sensitive intelligence of macaques and disambiguate artificial life from the lives lived by real nonhuman animals. Video documentation shows the iMac as not an intruder in the macaques' home but an object of fascination inviting cognitive engagement from these intensely curious writers. Indeed, the video indicates an appreciation for the monkey-computer *cognitive assemblage*, for its unpredictability, its gleeful hybridity, its playful philosophical implications. Coined by Nick Srnicek and further developed by Katherine Hayles over a series of texts, the term cognitive assemblage refers to a network of actants joined together through collaborative processes of cognition. Cognition is a practice enacted by humans, nonhuman animals, and technology, regardless of whether each collaborator possesses consciousness as we tend to understand it ("while all thinking is cognition, not all cognition is thinking" [Hayles, 2014: 201]). The Infinite Monkey Theorem, as both a philosophical toy and inspiration for a work of performance art, is ahead of its time – an over a century old proposal for a cognitive assemblage involving unthinking cognition, whether we attribute the unthought *just* to technology (the typewriter) or also, per usual, to the monkeys, as well.

1.3 On Chimera without the Counting of Feet

Shakespeare's poetry breathes sunshine and flowers; it flows with the freedom of a rippling brook, whereas [Francis] Bacon's few lines of verse show the careful student slowly and laboriously counting the feet in each line lest a misguided hexameter slip in among some unsuspecting pentameters.

William Joseph Radditz (1921: 101)

The form of the Infinite Monkey Theorem, in all its variations, describes a situation of writing that fuses organic and inorganic capabilities. In their recent edited volume on "synthetic cognition," Ilan Manouach and Anna Engelhardt embrace the idea of the chimera as a model for such hybrid intelligence. Indeed, for them, *all intelligence* is heterogeneous, a "combination of parts forming a unified entity" (2022: 10). "The 'synthetic' of chimerism shows that 'artificial' intelligence encompasses both humans and non-humans, welcoming the synthetic nature of intelligence itself" (2022: 12). Making a related point in the context of AI-generated visual art, Joanna Zylinska "proposes[s] to see different forms of human activity, including art, as having *always* been technical, and thus also, to some extent, artificially intelligent" (2020: 13). Writing is another activity that has always been technical (indeed, Jacques Derrida's critique of phonocentrism is also a claim for humans' originary technicity). The Infinite Monkey Theorem, which proposes a kinship between Shakespeare and a bio-technical writing apparatus (monkeys + typewriters) even when it ends up severing that relationship when the apparatus fails to produce, has played with the idea of writing as hybrid and artificially intelligent since long before Large Language Models (LLMs, systems trained on massive datasets with the goal of recognizing, classifying, translating, predicting, and/or generating texts). And long before the Theorem, "Shakespeare consciously practiced his own form of database" by collating and combining others' phrases, plots, and characters, a process modeled, perhaps, on the work of bees to make honey from nectar collected from different flowers (Stallybrass, 2007: 1581).

My understanding of the Infinite Monkey Theorem acknowledges the heterogeneity of all intelligence and relies on historical constructions of Shakespeare as both the pinnacle of *human* intellectual achievement and the receiver of *nonhuman* inspiration. Indeed, the Bard's genius has been frequently positioned throughout history as simultaneously supernatural and super natural. Despite the secularization of the Enlightenment (or perhaps because of it), the idea of genius based on such extraordinary men as Shakespeare and Homer retains some aspects of the mystical indicated by the word's etymology, as Darrin M. McMahon details in his book *Divine Fury: A History of Genius*. As the concept of genius developed throughout the seventeenth and eighteenth centuries, in large part to explain the creativity of Shakespeare despite his allegedly sub-par formal education, it came to be contrasted with the mere artfulness of the highly trained but derivative author (Bate, 1998: 161–163). Shakespeare the genius was both the recipient of supernatural gifts from something like an attending deity and a glorious bird tweeting artlessly in the British countryside between sips of the River Avon. Of course, neither genii nor songbirds really need classroom education. Shakespeare breathed and his poetry flowed freely; he did not laboriously count feet. Gary Taylor explains that "Eighteenth-century painters and poets had imagined baby Shakespeare, like baby Jesus, already instinct with godhead, being presented with the gifts of the Magi or suckled by buxom Muses" (1989: 174). Baby Jesus was at home amidst an ox and a donkey, Shakespeare might very well have been a furball nursing from a deific teat, and we have a holy trinity in the assemblage of genius, nature, and divinity.

The transcendentalizing of mortal genius continued in the nineteenth century. "With Romanticism," Jonathan Bate notes, "poetry was elevated into a form of secular scripture, Shakespeare into God" (Bate, 1998: 184). Criticism ensued. By 1847, the situation had so seriously chafed Søren Kierkegaard that he complained of the erosion of the boundary between geniuses and apostles in his bluntly titled "The Difference Between a Genius and an Apostle." "[G]ood night to Christianity," Kierkegaard sighs dramatically. "Brilliance [*Aandrighed*] and the spirit [*Aand*], revelation and originality, a call from God and genius, an apostle and a genius – all this ends up being just about one and the same" (1997: 93). Lacking Kierkegaard's histrionics and thus considerably less entertaining is a positive review of Richard Grant White's "Essay Towards the Expression of Shakespeare's Genius" (1865) that admits some nagging misgivings about the author's potential "indifferen[ce]" on the subject of the one true God ("Shakespeare," 1868: 27). White may be responsible for the best writing on Shakespearean genius ever published – better than Coleridge! – but he makes the sus move of positioning "Shakespeare in some sense among the divinities" ("Shakespeare," 1868: 27). McMahon follows this thread into the early-twentieth century, in which the cult of genius was under scrutiny for the spiritually redemptive role afforded the genius and the troubling fervor of those who devoted themselves to genii-poets or scientists. The widespread "worship of genius" was particularly fraught in Soviet Russia, in which "the question of religion in a state without religion" was bitterly controversial (McMahon, 2013: 203).

While Manouach and Engelhardt don't have the sacred in mind when they argue for synthetic intelligence, the historical emergence of Shakespeare as a genius of divine fury invites a broader discussion of nonhuman cognition than our current obsession with chatbots like ChatGPT would immediately suggest.[17] The Enlightenment portrait of the genius gripped by a creative frenzy heaven-sent, the Romantic idea of the genius creating unconsciously and without full comprehension, the early-twentieth century image of a monkey bashing a keyboard and accidentally writing a glorious sonnet, praise *Macaca nigra*, and the later-twentieth century proposition that *Hamlet* might just be the product of correlation matrices – however different they all are – are *rehearsals of the imagination* for twenty-first century visions of nonhuman textual production and synthetic intelligence. This is true whether what is produced is Shakespeare's *Hamlet* or Shakespeare-esque poetry with a recognizable style and voice, as with Shakespeare chatbots. Throughout dominant Anglophone cultural histories, Shakespeare has been at the center of questions of human capability that elevate but also challenge human agency. In other words, Shakespeare the genius can allow us to think through intelligence as chimeric, networked, and potentially nonconscious – albeit without comforting resolution.

The relevance of the Bard to discussions of the intelligence of the artificial and the artificiality of intelligence reasserts itself with every reference to Shakespeare in relation to LLMs, an almost daily accumulation that makes it difficult for me to know when to stop writing this volume about writing. Current popular discourse on ChatGPT and its rivals reinforces the idea that what is to be lost or gained is *Shakespeare*. Moreover, in opinion piece after opinion piece, affirmations of the dire stakes as well as criticism of unnecessary

---

[17] As much as I don't like to focus on the product of an individual corporation, "ChatGPT has had more coverage than any other AI topic in the last 40 years," in the words of Artificial General Intelligence researcher Aaron Turner (Scialom, 2023).

freakouts are routinely illustrated by the Infinite Monkey Theorem. *ChatGPT: Just the Infinite Monkey Theorem with a Modern Twist? / So to all you stupid monkeys, be afraid, be very afraid* (Yu, 2023). The figure of Shakespeare in the Infinite Monkey Theorem performs as an electrical magneto that powers speculation on the possibility of writing's dystopian future.

There is Google Bard, of course. In February of 2023, Google CEO Sundar Pichai released a statement introducing their ChatGPT competitor. Described as an "experimental conversational AI service, powered by LaMDA [Language Model for Dialogue Applications]," "Bard seeks to combine the breadth of the world's knowledge with the power, intelligence and creativity of our large language models" (Pichai, 2023). Google's parent company, Alphabet, reportedly lost $100 billion in market value after the release of a Twitter advertisement that shows Bard "spark[ing] a child's imagination about the infinite wonders of the universe" by mistakenly attributing the first images of exoplanets to the James Webb Space Telescope (Olson, 2023). An article about the scandal, titled "GPT or not GPT, that is the question: Bard blunder doesn't bode well for Google's ChatGPT killer," is illustrated with a stock image of Shakespeare as Hamlet fingering Yorick's skull. "The Bard of Avon himself was prone to the odd foible in his day too," author William Farrington reminds us, excusing Google Bard's whoopsie daisy. "In Julius Ceasar [sic], which takes place in Ancient Rome around 45 BC, Shakespeare makes reference to a clock striking on the hour. Mechanical clocks weren't invented until at least 1,600 years later." Google may have "tragically fubbed [sic]" an astronomy question, but Shakespeare himself was a minor fuck up, and look how great he is (Farrington, 2023).

Clearly preoccupied by the Bard's power as both a preternatural and distinctly human writer, social media posts and online essays about Generative AI obsessively recount prompts that reference Shakespeare. Hey, ChatGPT, "Recite Hamlet's famous monologue But change it to be from the Perspective of 10000 monkey's trying to recreate Shakespeare." The output includes the disappointing "To delete – to sleep, / To sleep, perchance to dream of Shakespeare."[18] Instead: "Pretend you are William

---

[18] www.reddit.com/r/shakespeare/comments/108g0mw/i_asked_chatgpt_to_re cite_hamlets_famous/.

Shakespeare and write an original speech about the dangers if [sic] AI in your traditional William Shakespeare style."[19] ChatGPT spins out the following: "Like the serpent in the garden of Eden, AI will tempt us with promises of ease and convenience . . . But be warned, for this knowledge comes with a price."[20] Within two months of the launch of the chatbot, there were over 14,000 references to Shakespeare and ChatGPT on Reddit, alone.[21] Remember that "Shakespeare," writes Pettman, "has merely rushed in to fill the vacuum left by the hasty departure of God," at least in humanist circles (2011: 18).

According to Michael Sag, a law professor who specializes in copyright issues and machine learning, "There's a saying that an infinite number of monkeys will eventually give you Shakespeare . . . There's a large number of monkeys here [with ChatGPT], giving you things that are impressive – but there is intrinsically a difference between the way that humans produce language, and the way that large language models do it" (qtd. in Sundar, 2023). And yet, blogger Kevin Dunn complains,

> A lot of people have been playing with ChatGPT and reporting back on all its hilarious mistakes. It makes logic errors. It bullshits its way through ignorance. It's surprisingly bad at math. It writes at a middle school level. Fine fine fine. This is all fair enough. But you could have said all the same things about Shakespeare at age six, and look where he ended up a few years later.[22]

Number of schools during Shakespeare's time with information available on the annual salary of the headmaster: 100. List of schools who paid their masters a greater annual salary than the master of the Stratford

---

[19] www.reddit.com/r/ChatGPT/comments/zfj1nj/chatgtp_warning_again st_ai_in_the_style_of/.

[20] www.reddit.com/r/ChatGPT/comments/zfj1nj/chatgtp_warning_again st_ai_in_the_style_of/.

[21] This number is based on a search conducted on January 27, 2023.

[22] jabberwocking.com/a-wee-warning-about-chatgpt/.

Grammar School: Ipswich, Oakham, Salisbury, Shrewsbury, Thame, Tiverton, Uppingham (Radditz, 1921: 53–56). What does this prove (allegedly, if not assuredly)?

> This assuredly is evidence of the high standard of education maintained at Shakespeare's school. This fact, coupled with the fact that Shakespeare spent 14,000 hours … at the Stratford Grammar School, under the guidance of three graduates of the world's greatest seat of learning, Oxford, certainly equipped him for the literary career which has justly marked him as the greatest literary genius of all time. (Radditz, 1921: 56–57)

Is today's Generative AI simply genius in training?

1.4 Oh, the Patriarchy of the Authentic Pen

Although my perspective on the Infinite Monkey Theorem is that of a media theorist, *Shakespeare and Nonhuman Intelligence* gains momentum from movements within Shakespeare studies to account for the action of the nonhuman in the circulation, consumption, and performance of Shakespeare's texts. Important for my purposes are approaches to Shakespeare that reconstitute the Shakespeare reader as the Shakespeare *user*, to borrow the title of a collection edited by Valerie M. Fazel and Louise Geddes. As they explain in their introduction, nonhuman users of Shakespeare include "algorithms, search engines, or collectively constructed social media timelines that reorganize and restructure Shakespeare to accommodate popular requests, machine-recognizable linguistic trends, or sponsored material" (2017: 8). The reconsideration of what reading means and who or what can be said to do it opens the discipline to an engagement with the "instances of technosocial communication that foreground the interplay of text, algorithms, and users" in the transformative consumption of "Shakespeare's" work (Jarrett and Naji, 2016). Shakespeare studies has responded to the insistently networked condition of Shakespeare's plays and sonnets (indeed, of all text) with applications of actor-network theory, new materialisms, object-oriented ontology, philosophy of technology, and, especially, media studies. These concerns register now familiar scholarly trends grouped together loosely as the posthumanities.[23]

Some recent developments in Shakespeare studies present the Bard and/ or his oeuvre as an assemblage or apparatus. This gesture to understand Shakespeare as a "shape-shifting system" moves us further away from a secure authoritative meaning (and, for some, from meaning altogether) (Hansen, 2017: 3). To wit, following the work of Douglas Lanier, scholars of appropriation have largely reconfigured their understanding of adaptation from a patrilineal arrangement emphasizing the new work's proximity to Shakespeare's so-called original text to a rhizomatic assemblage in which instantiations of Shakespeare make connections in all directions (Lanier, 2014). When understood as a rhizome, Shakespeare "can move across texts (intertexts), histories, and peoples, connecting his corpus to virtually anything" (Desmet et al., 2017: 4).

The richness of the rhizome's proliferating possibilities and the rise of the Shakespeare user as a more capacious replacement for the reader or actor have encouraged Shakespeare studies to consider the uses put to Shakespeare and "his" work outside of the fine arts, literature, and film. Research on such topics as Shakespearean fandom and the application of Shakespeare to business management training have largely moved beyond the binaries of faithful/ unfaithful and resistant/compliant that limit previous studies of adaptation and appropriation (although, as Christy Desmet, Natalie Loper, and Jim Casey remark in their introduction to the essay collection *Shakespeare/Not Shakespeare*, "Outside academia … the distinction between authentic and inauthentic Shakespeare is made and policed on a daily basis" [2017: 2]).

---

[23] Let us bracket the important distinction made by Richard Grusin (and others) between the nonhuman and the posthuman, with the latter's pernicious "post-" "entail[ing] a historical development from human to something after the human, even as it invokes the imbrication of human and nonhuman in making up the posthuman turn" (2015: ix). This difference is generally inoperative within Shakespeare studies, which includes the nonhuman within genealogies of posthumanism; moreover, it is rarely essential to characterizations of the posthumanities, even if it should be.

Alternatively, some Shakespeare scholarship turns to animal studies and/or ecocriticism as the primary means within the posthumanities to reposition the human. As Karen Raber implies, the best of this work goes beyond indexing the natural world as an obviously recurring trope within Shakespeare's oeuvre to propose new ways of thinking with and through anthrodecentrism, which is certainly my goal (2018: 12). Shakespeare's grip on the human within a literary studies of a recently bygone era makes the Bard especially valuable for a critique of humanism's subtension of the idea of an essential humanity. At the same time, Shakespeare's distinctly pre-Enlightenment point of view, framed by an only emerging humanism, can offer an alternative to the liberal humanism the posthumanities aim to critique, especially in regard to distinctions made between humans and the rest of the natural world. Indeed, Renaissance humanism has been presented as a premonition of much later developments in the posthumanities and the sciences.

Surprisingly, given these recent disciplinary shifts, the impact of Shakespeare on the STEM fields and popular science writing remains underexamined. While scholars make a case for the value of scientific literacy to literary studies, the invocation of Shakespeare by scientists themselves is generally not of their concern. Exceptions include Graham Holderness on the quotation of *Hamlet* in Stephen Hawking's book *The Universe in a Nutshell*; a sizable bibliography on psychoanalysis's obsession with Shakespeare, going back to a cranky 1927 essay on the "demi-science" of psychology's unseemly guttering of our divine bard; and Laura Estill's "Shakespeare and Disciplinarity," which tracks quotations of Shakespeare in academic journals outside of the humanities (Schelling, 1927; Holderness, 2005; Estill, 2017). In Estill's contribution, she notes that "As English became the de facto language of science, among other disciplines, Shakespeare became central to the English literary canon, which is how Shakespeare's ideas and phrases came to permeate English-language academic writing" (2017: 182). She also observes that "When Shakespeare is not the object of study but rather the lens through which another object of study is approached, his works can be turned to illuminate almost any topic," underscoring the pluripotential of Shakespeare discussed in recent adaptation studies (2017: 178).

Estill's stated interest is in "non-Shakespearean yet academic use of Shakespeare – a surprisingly large purview that has yet to be considered critically" (2017: 167). She offers several ways that these citations operate within academic discourse, prioritizing Pierre Bourdieu's concept of cultural capital throughout her argument. Locating recent references to Shakespeare in such journals as the *International Journal of Behavioral Medicine*, *The Journal of the American College of Dentists*, and *The Journal of Urology*, Estill notes that "it is unsurprising that Shakespeare quotations pepper academic writing, because his works are already oft-quoted in popular culture" (2017: 181). This is certainly true. Estill provides a helpful schema for classifying such unsurprising academic allusions to Shakespeare.

Although not incorrect in the context of the citations she collates, Estill's explanation should not be extended to account completely for writing by all scientists. Jeans, Eddington, and Dawkins, for example, all utilize Shakespeare in surprising ways. Sure, Eddington quotes *Hamlet* – "I could be bounded in a nutshell and count myself a king of infinite space" – but leaves out the kicker "were it not that I have bad dreams" (1928: 83). That said, he does so in the context of differentiating spatial from temporal infinity, with the latter eliciting a horror from the physicist that the former does not. Eddington, a devout Quaker later accused of "number mysticism" for his efforts to determine all physical laws solely through mathematics, employs Hamlet's alternating angst and overconfidence as a crude index of his own affective responses to the sickening boundlessness of our "infinite past" and the satisfying boundlessness of space (Eddington, 1928: 83; Stanley, 2005). While science writing activating sublime dread would fall out of favor in the aftermath of the atomic bomb, when scientists were eager to restore a comfortable faith in the STEM fields as a public good, this more philosophical approach would return with late-twentieth century authors like Carl Sagan, whose Pulitzer prize-winning *The Dragons of Eden: Speculations on the Evolution of Human Intelligence* quotes *The Tempest*, *Macbeth*, *King Lear*, and *Richard III* (1977). An explanation of these references that would distill them down to cultural cachet misses the nuance of the authors' metaphysical cosmology, a complexity present even when those authors are shoddy readers of *Hamlet*.

Of course, Estill's argument is designed to account for twenty-first century scholarly publications and not twentieth century mass market writing by scientists. What goes unmentioned, however, is the possibility that the uses of Shakespeare in such disciplines as dentistry and urology may have been influenced by a long tradition of popular science writing by academic scientists in which invocations of *Hamlet* serve a more interesting purpose than simply making the author sound smart through capital-C culture. More to my point here, the use of "decontextualized Shakespearean snippets" to "bolster the author's authority" by scientists who "might not have any understanding of the broader play from which they are quoting" – oof! allegations of unfaithfulness and inauthenticity – is itself worthy of further investigation, a consideration of inauthentic authorship and unfaithful authority that takes us beyond Bourdieu's cultural capital (Estill, 2017: 175, 176). Shakespeare, himself, has always had a distinctively ambivalent relationship to authorship and authority, as I have already mentioned. Efforts by Anti-Stratfordians to discredit Shakespeare, now fodder for eager conspiracy theorists who enjoy amateur cryptanalysis on the Internet, and the derivative nature of many of Shakespeare's plays make allusions to Shakespeare in scientific texts more thought-provoking than Estill's argument permits. Indeed, I maintain throughout that the Bard has proven to be particularly applicable to contentious conceptions of authorship in different discursive milieux – from genetic science and ID theory to computation. Each of these, in its own way, stages a scene of writing in which human agency is destabilized and/or anxiously, lovingly reaffirmed.

"the infinite monkey theorem means that for every monkey that could write out all of shakespeares written work theres another monkey who was like. a couple words off . do you think they would know how close they were." "A few ~~monkeys~~ people wrote their own Hamlets before that one dude wrote his, so honestly maybe."[24] And then there's Richard Grant White, writing in 1865: "The manner in which the name is spelled in the old records varies almost to the extreme capacity of various letters to produce a sound approximating to the name as we pronounce it. It appears as

---

[24] www.reddit.com/r/CuratedTumblr/comments/rl8x1h/my_brain_isnt_infini te_monkeys_on_typewriters_but/.

Chacksper, Shaxpur, Shaxper, Schaksper, Schakesper, Schakspere, Schakespeire, Schakespeyr, Shagspere, Saxpere, Shaxpere, Shaxpeare, Shaxsper, Shaxspere, Shaxespere, Shakspear, Shakspeere, Schakspear, Shackspeare, Shackespeare, Shackespere, Shakspyr, Shaksper, Shakespere, Shakyspere, Shakeseper, Shakespire, Shakespeire, Shakespear, Shakespeare, Shakaspeare: and there are other variations of its orthography" (qtd. in "Shakespeare," 1868: 21–22). Whatever the name of that one dude, around ten editions of his plays published before 1600 had no author identified at all, as was common practice at the time (Murphy, 2003: 22).

In addition to Estill's "Shakespeare and Disciplinarity," a notable exception to the trend of neglecting the "almost any topics" of the STEM fields is Galey's *The Shakespearean Archive: Experiments in New Media from the Renaissance to Postmodernity* and article "Networks of Deep Impression: Shakespeare and the History of Information," which later becomes Chapter 6 of the book. His influential work addresses, among other things, "the pattern of Shakespearean references made by cyberneticists and information theorists" (2014: 35). "How does the notion that Shakespeare's texts are somehow exceptional in all of literature," Galey asks, "function in scientific knowledge domains like information science, which value generalization over special cases?" (2010: 294). Perhaps by somehow rendering him as *both* a special case ("central to the English literary canon," in Estill's words) and a generalization, given what Galey describes as "information theory's claims for Shakespeare's unexceptionality" (2014: 219). Consider biologist Jacques Monod's 1959 diaristic note-to-self: "From the point of view of the theory of information, the works of Shakespeare, with the same number of letters and signs aligned at random by a monkey, would have the same value" (qtd. in Kay, 2000: 220). Shakespeare demoted.

Hold in your ears the sound of monkeys typing with brutal indifference as you consider a question from Lynne Bruckner and Dan Brayton in their introduction to *Ecocritical Shakespeare*. "Is the mythology of a pristine Shakespeare 'warbl[ing] his native Wood-notes wilde' – as Milton put it – in any way connected to the bygone pristine wilderness posited by nostalgic environmentalism?" (2016: 2). We might reorient this question, left unanswered in Brayton and Bruckner's work, as the following: How is Shakespeare's particular genius considered so exceptional as to place his written expression within the lifeworld of the nonhuman? Back up. Could an exceptional man be an unexceptional bird who produced information no more valuable than that of an unexceptional monkey? Alan Turing throws out two numbers: M and N. M is the number of seconds a bird might take to raze Mount Everest grain by lithic grain, a duty performed once a year, while 1/N is the chance that a piece of chalk might fly out of his grip "and write a line of Shakespeare on the board before falling to the ground" (J. L. Britton, qtd. in Galey, 2010: 215). That swallow is not a swallow. Maybe Shakespeare is less a bird than the air that holds the bird aloft. "The universal genius of our great poet": air, "bearing without an effort in its broad bosom the great globe itself" (Kenny, 1864: 111).

The turn towards the Shakespeare user registers the openness of Shakespeare studies to account for unconventional applications of the Bard, even if the STEM fields have been underexplored. That said, the term *user* is generally employed as a replacement for *reader* or *performer* of Shakespeare's plays – not *writer*, as is my concern. This is clear in the introduction to the edited volume *The Shakespeare User*, which acknowledges the rise of Web 2.0, yet shows little interest in the writing component of read-write media necessary for the shift from consumption to prosumption that heralds the World Wide Web's second generation. But what is Turing's chalk doing in the above scenario? Of course, it is writing. More broadly, what does the volume's Shakespeare user have to say about a technosocial situation in which ChatGPT can wax, "To type, or not to type, that is the question"? and "10,000 monkeys trying to recreate Shakespeare" through a LLM can collectively whimper, "The undiscovered words and phrases/No monkey has typed before, puzzles the will."[25]

A more aggravating problem is the edited volume's wavering commitment to the nonhuman. Despite its anthrodecentric introduction, most essays in the collection ignore the possibility of a nonhuman reader, writer, or performer entirely by restricting the purview of user to "readers, playgoers, media consumers, researchers, and instructors: anyone who has an affinity for Shakespeare, and a desire to understand his works and the four centuries of artistic expression they have inspired," as does Erik M. Johnson (2017: 187).

---

[25] www.reddit.com/r/ChatGPT/comments/108fps2/10_000_monkeys_hamlet/.

Does Turing or his chalk or a TikTok hashtag necessarily have a desire to understand Shakespeare's works? What about the rhesus macaque identified as "Monkey J," who successfully typed "To be or not to be. That is the question." (periods and all, two spaces after the first period) in 2016 using a surgically implanted brain-computer interface designed as an experimental prototype for people with paralysis?[26]

Is it true that "anything that moves can write or be made to write"?

> If, the logic goes, even women are capable of learning to type, perhaps even an ape could type something meaningful such that we could not tell it apart from Shakespeare. Even more radically ... a truly random letter generator would be capable of such a feat, given infinite time. The patriarchy of the authentic pen in this logic is clear. In short, if all it takes to inscribe meaning on a recording surface is a series of key oscillations between two positions within a circulation, then anything that moves can write or be made to write. (Nail, 2019: 435)

So goes philosopher Thomas Nail's brief analysis of the Infinite Monkey Theorem as an index of "a new typographic subject whose graphic motions become fused with the writing machine itself and thus increasingly anonymous." Such "kinographic logic" shuttles into the future with awe-inspiring boldness to live its best damn life "in the computer revolution of the later twentieth century" (Nail, 2019: 435).

Desperately resisting this kinographic logic in a *New York Times* opinion piece, Maureen Dowd claims that "Chat GPT is typing, not writing." For now. Her "A.I.: Actually Insipid Until It's Actively Insidious" (a most unnerving title anticipating the *Sturm und Drang* of LLMs' teenage years) is illustrated by a benday dotted image of Shakespeare's face from the Chandos painting disintegrating into zeros and ones – or, when read from left to write, binary digits consolidating into a familiar portrait. Shakespeare

---

[26] Information about this project, led by Stanford University-based engineer Krishna Shenoy, is available at www.youtube.com/watch?time_continue=51&v=nxD2KDq18_E&feature=emb_logo.

is top center, as always, the face of writing coming face to face with a chatbot (Dowd, 2023). And in this face off, Shakespeare does not move. Shakespeare never moves – he composes. Picture George Henry Hall's triptych *Shakespeare Composing While Looking Outward* (1894).[27] In all three paintings, the Bard has a thousand-yard stare and a quill held aloft, hovering above the page. He bears without effort, without artifact. Shakespeare is air. The feather is borne.

And yet, *he writes?*

Shakespeare and Nonhuman Intelligence offers a third proposition: **the Infinite Monkey Theorem uses Shakespeare to advance arguments about writing (that are also arguments about chance and life and the universe that are also arguments about the human, the animal, the technological, and the sacred).** Let me now borrow from W. B. Worthen's bang-up analysis of Annie Dorsen's *A Piece of Work* (2013), a performance for a human actor, synthesized speech, projected words, lights, and fog in which the text of Shakespeare's *Hamlet* is subjected to various algorithmic procedures. As I repurpose Worthen: the Infinite Monkey Theorem stages writing as a device "for framing human 'interiority'," a device that itself is part   of "a technical system that conventionally identifies Shakespearean writing not merely as a sign of the human, but as an algorithm for its production," a device, I would add, that is unstable (2020: 201). In other words, the Infinite Monkey Theorem is a small anthropogenic machine for playing with the big idea of human interiority that allows us to see the even bigger anthropogenic machine that is writing. And here, writing should be understood most broadly as potentially scriptural (divine), replicate and reproductive (biological), and algorithmic (technological) (although, as this volume proceeds, it will become clear that these are not mutually exclusive categories). Writing is both a human and nonhuman textual practice, writing is conscious, nonconscious, and unconscious, writing is chimeric – else it would not serve the ambivalence of the anthropogenic machine. Put differently, a metaphysics of the non/human is inherently a *graphic project*.

---

[27] This image can be viewed here: commons.wikimedia.org/wiki/File: Shakespeare_composing_while_looking_outward_(Hall, 1894).jpg.

Yes, the "dumb typewriter" still writes (and ableism abounds in discussions of intelligence). See here "an example of a monkey at a typewriter vs. a monkey at a computer keyboard":

> If the monkey types at random on a typewriter, the probability that it types out all the works of Shakespeare (assuming the text is 1 million bits long) is $2^{-1,000,000}$. If the monkey sits at a computer terminal, however, the probability that it types out Shakespeare is now $2^{-K \text{ (Shakespeare)}} \approx 2^{-250,000}$, which though extremely small is still exponentially more likely than when the monkey sits at a dumb typewriter. The example indicates that a random input to a computer is much more likely to produce "interesting" outputs than a random input to a typewriter. We all know that a computer is an intelligence amplifier. Apparently it creates sense from nonsense as well. (Cover and Thomas, 1991: 162)

What scene of writing is this?

Despite its massive popularity amongst information theorists (see above), programmers, math lovers, atheists, Christian fundamentalists, and the social mediasphere at large, the Infinite Monkey Theorem has been mentioned by Shakespeare studies very rarely and only in passing. I have found only one reference by a Shakespeare scholar, and that is in Galey's *The Shakespearean Archive*. The Theorem is, I believe, a missed opportunity to consider Shakespeare's relation to a broadly accommodating idea of writing as non/human intelligence and to place products of machine learning like ChatGPT and Google Bard within more wide-ranging conversations about randomness, agency, creativity, and divine will.

1.5 Astrobiologist Cautions against Jumping the Gun

This volume offers non/human intelligence as a more expansive frame for artificial writing than AI. Non/human intelligence, as an operative category, brings Shakespeare's oeuvre, typing monkeys, DNA, and computation together with sacred writing. This category comes into better focus in

Section 2, in which I give sustained attention to a lengthy conversation yet unregistered by Shakespeare studies: the conscription of the Bard, the Infinite Monkey Theorem, and information science into proofs of the existence of a transcendental creator within discourse on ID. My choice to access non/human writing through a theological discussion is less jarring if one acknowledges the spirituality of modern and contemporary technoculture (think Silicon Valley's obsession with various gnostic and nonwestern religions), molecular biology (with its explicitly Christian metaphors, as will later become clear), and pop astrophysics (which tends to turn mystical). An examination of the longstanding philosophical problem of non/human writing suggests that neither genius nor science has completely replaced god, however we understand this entity. Instead, the notion of supernatural intelligence is always present in anthropogenic machines of all kinds, either implicitly or explicitly, as ghost or gear, haunting the secular, driving the sacred.

Shakespeare and Nonhuman Intelligence contributes to the "rising literature on the relationship between religion and digital culture," scholarship that focuses on "the supernatural as a locus in which particular forms of imagination and modalities of interaction with digital media are constructed" (Natale and Pasulka, 2020: 3). This body of knowledge was anticipated by such major players in the development of information science as Norbert Wiener, whose popular science book *God and Golem, Inc.: A Comment on Certain Points Where Cybernetics Impinges on Religion* attempts to find "vital common ground where science and religion come together" through a critique of the "layers of prejudice" endemic to both practices as well as a philosophical inquiry into the ontology of computers (Wiener, 1964: 4). Although Wiener would entirely disapprove of theories of ID, his defense of putting "creative activity under one heading, and in not parceling it out into separate pieces belonging to God, to man, and to the machine" has surprising relevance to a theist discourse that uses the computer programmer and the poet as pedagogical models for the intelligent, divine creator (1964: 1, 95).

The specific argument made about Shakespeare, computation, and the supernatural by ID adherents will be detailed in Section 2. For now, let me spend some time with the vague idea of intelligence in ID theory by way of an oblique reference to the Infinite Monkey Theorem: prolific ID researcher William Dembski's snark that "Perhaps Shakespeare was a genius. Perhaps

Shakespeare was an imbecile who just by chance happened to string together a long sequence of apt phrases" (2004: 122). The binary between genius and so-called imbecile (seen already in the distinction between intelligence amplifier and dumb typewriter), finds an easy analog in the Theorem's preliminary separation of Shakespeare and monkeys in a scene of writing. This binary is a pattern that reappears throughout discourse on ID. For example, engineer of the ID movement and former University of California, Berkeley law professor Phillip Johnson, when asked to define ID, offers the following:

> There are two hypotheses to consider scientifically. One is you need a creative intelligence to do all the creating that has been done in the history of life; the other is you don't, because we can show that unintelligent, purposeless, natural processes are capable of doing and actually did do the whole job.

Johnson clarifies that "if non-intelligence couldn't do the whole job, then intelligence had to be involved in some way."[28] Given the language and structure of this explanation, ID's intense fascination with the Infinite Monkey Theorem – usually referenced in more explicit terms than Dembski does in the earlier quotation – is unsurprising. It also tracks that arguments against ID would engage with the Theorem as well. A diagram that divides *and* joins the so-called "unintelligent, purposeless" kinetics of natural creatures from/with Shakespearean creative genius can be incorporated into multiple worldviews.

A redirection of Biblical creationism, ID got its name from Charles Thaxton, a physical chemist and editor of the high school textbook *Of Pandas and People: The Central Question of Biological Origins* (1989). In the middle of writing the book, creationism was outlawed from US public school science curricula as a result of the Supreme Court case *Edwards* v. *Aguillard* (1987). Needing a term that lacked the theological associations of *creation*,

---

[28] This interview with Phillip Johnson is available at www.pbs.org/wgbh/nova/id/defense-id.html#:~:text=Phillip%20Johnson%20is%20known%20as,including%20humans%2C%20came%20into%20being.

Thaxton chose *Intelligent Design*, repurposing lingo used by a NASA scientist, presumably in relation to the Search for Extraterrestrial Intelligence (SETI) (Witt, 2007).

Despite claims to the contrary, the essential similarities between ID and creationism were key rhetorical players in the landmark case *Kitzmiller* v. *Dover Area School District* (2004), in which a district court struck down a policy requiring teachers to address ID and use *Of Pandas and People* as a reference. In the course of preparing for the trial, Kitzmiller witness Barbara Forrest discovered a word-processing error – "cdesign proponent-sists," "a textual transitional fossil" demonstrating the creationist aims of the textbook's authors. A mistake in replacing "creationists" with "design proponents" in a draft of *Of Pandas and People*, "cdesign proponentsists" exposes the indissoluble connection between creationism and ID (Scott and Matzke, 2007: 8674). At its inception, ID is a new "science" built on a secret foundation of old creationism, revealed in successive variants of a document. Despite the fallout from the Kitzmiller trial, ID continues its attempts to distinguish itself from its predecessor based on the capacious-ness of the notion of Intelligent Designer – which could technically be the Christian God or some generic divine actor or even an extraterrestrial – as well as ID's reportedly more systematic and objective methodologies.

An interest in extraterrestrials, if perhaps only for rhetorical purposes, is common within ID discourse. The online column *Mind Matters News*, which offers "Breaking and noteworthy news from the exciting world of natural and artificial intelligence" and is sponsored by the primary institu-tion for ID research, brings together stories on the search for extraterres-trial life, machine learning, robotics, animal behavior, neuroscience, and mathematics. In the publication's "Astrobiologist Cautions Against Jumping the Gun in Spotting ET," alien communication is defined as requiring "specified complexity," an idea explained with recourse to Shakespeare (brackets in the original):

> A long sequence of random letters is complex without being specified [it is hard to duplicate but it also doesn't mean anything]. A short sequence of letters like "so," is specified without being complex. [It means something but what it

means is not very significant by itself]. A Shakespearean
sonnet is both complex and specified. [It is both complex and
hard to duplicate and it means a lot in a few words]
(*Astrobiologist Cautions*, 2021)

Identified here as part of information theory but more accurately attributed
to Dembski, the concept of specified complexity is central to design theory
and is repeatedly defined throughout the literature using virtually the same
language.[29] The usual example given is a Shakespearean sonnet. Specified
complexity requires authorship, whether that author is God, Shakespeare,
or ET. A similar explanation of specified complexity by Dembski acolyte
David F. Coppedge swaps the sonnet for a play, contrasting the simple
formation of a snow crystal, however beautiful, with the complex poetry of
Romeo and Juliet. Unlike DNA or an alien radio signal, Coppedge's snowflakes are not definitively designed by an intelligent agent. "If the snowflakes landed on a fence rail and spelled out the line from Shakespeare," he
imagines, perhaps unwittingly recalling Turing's chalk, "that would be
something else entirely" (Coppedge, 2021). Writing, we have, again,
nonhuman writing.

Charles Babbage, inventor of a famously failed but discursively successful nineteenth century analog computer, offers a precedent to later entan-
glements of science, Shakespeare, textuality, and the Christian God.
Babbage's fascinating "The Ninth Bridgewater Treatise" challenges the
seeming incompatibility of Genesis and scientific discovery through
a reminder that the Bible lacks the kind of contextual information that
helps us understand, let's say, Shakespeare's works. As an analogy, he
conjures an apocalypse of the Anglophone canon in which only one manuscript of one Shakespeare play remains and all literary works by
Shakespeare's contemporaries, as well as all subsequent English literature
till nearly the present day, have been destroyed. Babbage continues:

[29] According to Sahotra Sakar, "what Dembski means by 'information' does not
correspond to either of these two standard notions" of information: the semantic
or the statistical (Sakar, 2007: 119, 120).

Under such circumstances, what would be our knowledge of Shakespeare? We should undoubtedly understand the general tenor and the plots of his plays. We should *read* the language of all his characters; and viewing it generally, we might even be said to understand it. But how many words connected with the customs, habits, and manners of the time must, under such circumstances, necessarily remain unknown to us! ... Such I conceive to be the view which common sense bids us take of the interpretation of the book of Genesis. (Babbage, 1837)

The engineer's approach to scripture acknowledges its ambiguity by attending to its fragile materiality (as documents that can be "annihilated") and its textuality (with some relationship to "the language of the Hebrews" of the present but inscribed so far in the past that it provides no firm argument against scientific empiricism) (Babbage, 1837). While Babbage may at first seem to call into question the trustworthiness of Biblical accounts of creation, instead, he attempts to challenge readers' certainty of them, opening exegesis to a hopeful skepticism that allows for the possibility that geology and Genesis might be saying exactly the same thing after all. Ever the theist, Babbage is later embraced by both creation scientists and proponents of ID as a model Christian STEM practitioner, although the simple fact of his strong religious beliefs overshadows the specificity of his argument. Surprisingly, Babbage also inspired Darwin in the development of the naturalist's theory of speciation (Gere, 2012: 14).

While the ID community is happy to place itself within an eminent techno-spirituo-scientific lineage including Babbage and his analytical engine, it usually attempts to distance itself from creationist Bible studies, for legal reasons. Instead, scripture is typically replaced by the idea of textuality more broadly, although not named as such. For example, *Of Pandas and People* explains the notion of an intelligent cause with the support of a photograph of "JOHN LOVES MARY" inscribed in sand. If we were to encounter such a love note on a beach, experience tells us that an intelligent agent must have written it. The same experience underwrites genetic science as well, they say. "When we find a complex message coded into the nucleus of a cell, it is reasonable to draw the same conclusion" (Davis and Kenyon, 1996: 7). Here, the textbook is referring to DNA as complex specified textual information like *Romeo and Juliet* and Shakespeare's sonnets.

For supporters of ID, if DNA is the Book of Life, a common metaphor in molecular biology and its popularization, then it must have an intelligent author. A realization of the textuality of DNA – through a 1981 academic paper that argues for "a structural identity between the nucleotide sequences in DNA and the alphabetical letter sequences in a book," as Thaxton summarizes – provides the Eureka moment early on in Thaxton's reconfiguration of embattled creationism into what he hoped would be a legally triumphant discourse (qtd. in Witt, 2007). It is the understanding of DNA as writing that helps him connect nucleotide sequencing to intelligence. If the string of DNA base pairs and written text "are mathematically identical and I know that intelligence is responsible for the alphabetical letter sequence, then I'm on safe ground when I say that intelligence is responsible for the sequencing of the nucleotides" (qtd. in Witt, 2007).

DNA has been folded into the ID worldview – and the scriptural so thoroughly submerged in their idea of the textual – in large part because genetic research has long invoked the Book of Life. Lily E. Kay provides a provocative critique of the "scriptural genomic visions" that accompany this metaphor in her book *Who Wrote the Book of Life?: A History of the Genetic Code*. As she explains, the idea of the genetic Book of Life developed in the 1960s through the influence of information theory on both linguistics and biology. In a series of questions that would certainly grab followers of ID, Kay writes,

> While the power of the metaphor also inheres in its affinities to the sublime, few molecular biologists would assign authorship of the genomic Book of Life to God; though they may regard its content – information – as an ontological entity, even a cosmological principle. Thus the Book of Life leads back to the age-old conundrum of creation versus revelation: In the beginning was the Word? If the genome was written, what is the source of this writing, what is its agency and its materiality? (2000: xvi–xvii)

Through a mid-century textualization of the genome, the genetic code came to be understood as a "scriptural technology" – despite the "paradoxes of speechless communication, authorless writing, and the act of (re) creation as revelation" (Kay, 2000: 5, 7). The perplexity of the metaphor was not lost on Claude Lévi-Strauss. In a 1967 debate with linguist Roman Jakobson, biologist François Jacob, and geneticist Philippe L'Héritier, the anthropologist probes, "Can there be a prediscursive knowledge of language existing prior to its construction by humans? Could there be something, as biologists claim, which resembles the structure of language but which involves neither consciousness nor subject?" (in Kay, 2000: 34). ID proponents would say that while a prediscursive language may not have been constructed by humans, it must have been made by a conscious intelligent agent (which, strictly speaking, could be an alien or god). Although Kay does not mention ID, we could insert it into her history: perhaps genetic science was hoisted with its own petard when it chose the Biblical metaphor of the Book of Life. Molecular biology, long "suffused with theistic images and religious icons," would find its shadow in the theistic religion of ID "science" (Kay, 2000: 36).

To wit, we have St. John: "In the beginning was the Word . . . ." So opens Edward N. Trifonov and Volker Brendel's *Gnomic: A Dictionary of Genetic Codes*, published three years before *Of Pandas and People*. The authors' word processing program didn't recognize the word "genomic," suggesting "gnomic" as a replacement (1986: 3). Gnomic it is. In a preface that mentions Goethe, Faust, St. John (again), and the "hieroglyphs of nucleotide sequences," the bioinformatics researchers playfully explain the aptness of the mistake. "'Gnomic' means 'wise and pithy, expressive, full of meaning' – all certainly attributes of the language of genes" (1986: 3). Gnomes are supernatural earth-dwellers identified by Renaissance polymath Paracelsus; Trifonov and Brendel liken them to the homunculi Leeuwenhoek believed he saw crouching shamefully inside human spermatozoa (surely these funny little men communicate in arcana) (1986: 7). The precursor to Trifonov and Brendel's dictionary is a 1965 publication of "the text of the first 'tablet' of Gnomic extracted from yeast cells" (1986: 7). That alphabet has four letters, each a simplified chemical structural formula of a particular nucleotide. "Bearing in mind the importance of information contained in these texts on living matter, its functions and malfunctioning, one could envision that Gnomic will soon become a most intensively studied language," although a complete "gnomology," the authors predict, is for the distant future (1986: 8).

Words, authorship, Shakespeare, and the atheists' allegedly all too desperate clutching: disagreeing with ID is supposedly "like insisting that Shakespeare was not written by Shakespeare because it might have been written by a billion monkeys sitting at a billion keyboards typing for a billion years. So it might. But the sight of scientific atheists clutching at such desperate straws has put new spring in the step of theists" (Clifford Longley qtd. in Meyer, 2001: 65). Burn. *Historic Doubts Respecting Shakespeare; Illustrating Infidel Objections against the Bible* (1848), theist argument by irony, as summarized by Gary Taylor: "If you doubted the authority of the Bible, why should you believe in the existence of God or Jesus? If you could not trust the Bible, why should you trust the First Folio? And if you doubted the authority of the First Folio, why should you believe in the existence of that incarnate deity of poetry, the 'immortal' Shakespeare?" "[D]efend[ing] the historicity of Jesus Christ against the objections of atheists by facetiously demonstrating that the skeptics' objections could just as easily be leveled against the existence of Shakespeare," this argument continues to echo in ID circles over 150 years later, but with Biblical references usually conspicuously removed (Taylor, 1989: 2013).

Design theory presents itself as not theology but science, albeit heterodox and repressed, despite professions of love from springy devoted theists and Bible literalists. For my purposes, it is not important that ID is not valid science, or, for that matter, that Infinite Monkeyphiles on social media may not all understand mathematical ideas of probability, some scientists may not have read the whole Shakespeare play from which they quote, and nineteenth century Baconians obsessed with disproving Shakespearean authorship were failed cryptologists. What matters to me here is the *use* of science, however poor, however loving, however offhand, however rhetorical, however justified, however unjust. And the use of Shakespeare. Together.

1.6 A Shakesperotics of Intelligence

This volume is my own contribution to "Shakesperotics" – which, as coined by Gary Taylor in his impressive but unerotic *Reinventing Shakespeare*, "embraces everything that a society does in the name – variously spelled – of Shakespeare" (1989: 6). The Infinite Monkey Theorem is a single fine but long thread within the warp and weft of a "subject so big that it has no name" (or none until Taylor made one up) (1989: 6). Surprisingly, despite his insistence that "the history of Shakespeare's evolving reputation must incorporate the annals of criticism, the theatre, and many other disciplines" in the embrace of everything, Taylor restricts himself almost exclusively to the business of people who have the usual business with Shakespeare – editors, publishers, directors, actors, literary critics, scholars, and creative writers like James Joyce and Virginia Woolf (1989: 6). But what about the many other disciplines that have no business quoting Shakespeare, or rather, no obvious or expected business? How do scientists, theologians, and computer programmers operate what Taylor calls "the mechanisms of [Shakespeare's] cultural renown" (1989: 6)? How do these mechanisms come together in the anthropogenic machine?

Shakespeare and Nonhuman Intelligence adopts two primary approaches to the Monkey/Shakespeare problem – one broad and one narrow. First, it offers a kind of variorum of the Infinite Monkey Theorem over the past hundred years. Distributed throughout this volume are many references to the Theorem, often with only subtle variations in language but significant differences in context, interpretation, and valence. Some are from published books and academic articles and others from Reddit and Twitter. Some are from Darwin haters and others from AI skeptics. Despite my commitment to a wide range of monkeys, Section 2 is quite focused. It is devoted to an almost 40-year debate between theists and atheists about Shakespeare simulations by Richard Dawkins and, to a lesser extent, Richard Hardison. Their programs mobilize imaginary monkeys and lines from *Hamlet* to illustrate an important concept in the theory of evolution frequently misunderstood by theist critics of Darwin's ideas. The spectacular drama between design theory and evolutionary science in books, on social media, and in courtrooms exposes the anthropogenic machine in its most unguarded and vulnerable form, and thus deserves a section mostly of its own. Although I closely read this particular conversation, I also introduce other citations of the Theorem as the section unfolds. Section 3 functions as a conclusion. It turns to two twenty-first century monkey simulators, one of which did successfully generate the works of Shakespeare – finally, controversially – and then gets us back to ChatGPT and its "large monkey army" (always, as if we ever really left them all behind).[30]

All three sections address the ways in which the "innumerable interactions that (re)create Shakespeare through ongoing, dynamic processes" of "a dense, layered, interconnected network of parts" – as Claire Hansen puts it – include efforts *to (re)create Shakespeare in the most tragicomically literal of fashions* (2017: 3). This direct approach to (re)creation has been neglected by Shakespeare studies that view culture as a network but ignore one of the most ubiquitous examples of a Shakespearean assemblage. A more limited but nonetheless important concern of *Shakespeare and Nonhuman Intelligence* is to bring the critically neglected early digital humanities practitioner William Bennett, Jr. into a discussion of Shakespeare and computation. Getting to Bennett the physicist through physicists Jeans and Eddington, as I have done here, allows me to tell a new story, however briefly, of the development of humanities computing.

Moreover, although this is not the focus of *Shakespeare and Nonhuman Intelligence*, I offer the Infinite Monkey Theorem as a theory of computation, *with or without computers*, and not just a potentially computable problem. This theory is a force that gathers together Shakespeare the genius with conceptions of both writing and molecular genetics as technics of computation. Such an idea isn't so surprising in light of a claim by Marvin Minsky and Seymour Papert in their classic machine learning text *Perceptrons*, originally published in 1969.[31] Trailblazers of AI, Minsky and Papert introduce their book on neural networks (a category that would later include LLMs) as building the foundation for a "general theory of

---

[30] news.ycombinator.com/item?id=35412394.

[31] *Perceptrons* was revised and republished, with charming handwritten edits, in 1972, published again in 1988, with an added preface and epilogue, and then reissued with a new foreword in 2017.

computation" of interest to "psychologists and biologists who would like to know how the brain computes thoughts and how the genetic program computes organisms" (2017: 1). The allegedly computational nature of cognition and phenotypy – a reminder of the historical relationship between AI research and neuroscience and between computer science and biology – partially accounts for the applicability of monkey/ Shakespeare programs to discussions of the capabilities of humans who write, AI that writes, and the biological mechanisms that print the Book of Life.

An issue that will remain purposefully undeveloped in this volume is how to define intelligence. I think it's best to follow the lead of the fields of AI and design theory, both of which employ notoriously amorphous and unstable definitions of intelligence. Whatever notion of intelligence is being explicitly or implicitly invoked by references to ChatGPT or monkeys or Shakespeare or a divine creator, I propose that ideas of intelligence in the context of the Infinite Monkey Theorem have long helped us work through the tense relationship between human and more-than-human capabilities. Here, I want to take up a provocative claim by James Bridle in his book *Ways of Being: Animals, Plants, Machines: The Search for a Planetary Intelligence* – AI can be considered to be "a kind of guide to understanding the more-than-human intelligences which surround us" (2022: 82). Likewise, the Infinite Monkey Theorem is a kind of guide to understanding our ways of approaching several modes of more-than-human intelligence, even when alignments between humans and nonhumans are unsatisfying, temporary, failed, even if human exceptionalism is championed in the end, even when the exact nature of intelligence is frustratingly unclear.

Caleb Scharf captures the discomfiting ambivalence of our relationship with some kinds of more-than-human intelligence in *The Ascent of Information: How Data Rules the World* (tagline on the back cover: "Your information has a life of its own, and it's using you to get what it wants." (2021)). Repeatedly returning to Shakespeare in order to define his key terms, Scharf explains his concept of the *dataome* – "all of the non-genetic data we carry externally and internally" – through an anecdotal telling of his visit to Stratford-upon-Avon as well as a mathematical estimation of the energy demands of "the simple act of human arms raising and lowering copies of Shakespeare's writings" throughout history (2021: 6, 26). "[A]s we look at these numbers, and the myriad offshoots of objects and activities, I think it is impossible not to feel that Shakespeare's output has also taken on a burdensome life of its own, propagating itself into the future and compelling all of us to support it … " (2021: 28). Nonetheless, Shakespeare's poetry "represents only a single drop in a vast ocean of seemingly ethereal human-made data that nonetheless has an extremely tangible effect on us. That ocean, as we'll see, is both the glory and millstone of *Homo sapiens*" (2021: 28). For Scharf, the glorious but burdensome dataome is an intelligent, living system that grows and evolves through time, one that shapes and is shaped by biological systems.

Scharf's analysis is anthrodecentric. Like DNA, one conceptual model for the non/human capabilities of Sharf's dataome, data replicates. Data transforms. Data endures. In a way, data lives. And, although Scharf doesn't use this word, data *performs*. Indeed, we might apply his insight into the intelligent, agential life of data to a consideration of the subject of this series of Cambridge Elements: Shakespeare Performance. Thus far, I have argued that Shakespeare *performs* a function within the toy anthropogenic machine of the Infinite Monkey Theorem. And he does. However, I want to return to a term I used earlier: *reanimation*. If Shakespeare's textual output is also living data that performs at timescales in excess of human lifespans, we might also say that Shakespeare is continually *reanimated* by the dataset of Shakespearean performances, texts, derivatives, and successors, including Shakespeare-esque poetry written by bots and references to Shakespeare in the Infinite Monkey Theorem. Instead of Shakespeare in performance or even data about Shakespeare performance, we have Shakespeare reanimated by data that itself performs, as a puppet (Shakespeare) is repeatedly brought to life by a puppeteer (the Shakespeare dataset). Returning to this idea in Section 3, I follow anthropologists Teri Silvio, Paul Manning, and Ilana Gershon by offering animation – in our case, rather, reanimation – as a new critical paradigm for the twenty-first century.

Performance and animation are not mutually exclusive concepts. That said, Shakespeare Reanimation is the non/human turn of a publication series on Shakespeare Performance. Reanimation accounts for what the anthropogenic assemblage of monkeys and typewriters is designed to do – produce the human from what the human is not, again and again. Moreover, through its connection to dark magic and horror lore, reanimation reminds us of the anxiety triggered by a Theorem that decenters human agency through uncanny writing, be it a stand-in for the human genome, God's living word, stochastically generated text, or alien signals. Reanimation better accommodates the threat and promise of subjectless yet intelligent communication preoccupying our spirituo-bioinformatic age.

2 A Sequence of Possibilities Enabled by Various Couplings

2.1 Randomizing Alphabet Then Write Hamlet, Keeping

Jeans starts with the sun. It shrugged off parts of itself, he writes. "In the course of time, we know not how, when, or why, one of these cooling fragments gave birth to life" (1930/38: 13). And from there, eventually, from creatures Jeans imagines live only to multiply and die, eventually emerged the kind of lives focused on "emotions and ambitions," "aesthetic appreciations," and "religions in which their highest hopes and noblest aspirations lie enshrined" – concerns that "all seem equally foreign" to an indifferent universe (1930/38: 13, 14). We are but accidents. "The use of such a word need not imply any surprise that our earth exists, for . . . every conceivable accident is likely to happen in time" (1930/38: 14). Including a singular accident in which six simian typographic (non) subjects hammer away anonymously at machines for millions upon millions of years, and one churns out a sonnet by Shakespeare amid untold pages of froth. Jeans is an astrophysicist, and so he gets to Shakespeare and religion from celestial bodies. But we will now turn away from the sublime improbability of our cosmological beginnings to another grand situation of chance and consequence – that of the diversification of terrestrial life and the biomolecular operations of DNA, the latter unknown to scientists of Jeans's day. In other words, let's get to the tragicomedy of Shakespeare and religion and monkeys and gibberish not from astrophysics but from *biology*.

Richard Dawkins is certainly the most widely known evolutionary biologist in the world. Bestselling author, popularizer of a gene-centered approach to evolution, coiner of the word "meme," and infamously outspoken atheist, Dawkins created a computer program he calls "the monkey/

Shakespeare model" for his book *The Blind Watchmaker* (1986/2015: 72). This philosophical toy uses the Infinite Monkey Theorem to illustrate the difference between two types of selection as they relate to evolutionary change. It is important to note that although Dawkins and his ilk are called Darwinists by creationists and ID adherents, it is more accurate to call them Neo-Darwinists. Neo-Darwinism, otherwise known as the Modern Synthesis, combines Darwin's theory of evolution with Gregor Mendel's ideas on inheritance. As the synthetic theory of evolution developed over the course of the twentieth century, it incorporated insights from genetics and later, molecular biology. The most important discovery for our purposes is the Central Dogma of molecular biology, which states, in its most basic form, that information flow in biological systems (almost always) moves from DNA to RNA to proteins.[32] In other words, DNA has instructions for producing proteins: the DNA serves as a template for the process of transcription that creates messenger RNA, and this mRNA is involved in a process of translation that codes for amino acids, which are combined to make proteins. The references to proteins like hemoglobin in *The Blind Watchmaker* indicate a Neo-Darwinist worldview in which the relationship between evolution, genetics, and the production of the most broadly important functional molecules in our bodies is well established.

So here we are: the popular science book *The Blind Watchmaker*, which continues to be taken apart and reconstructed in debates on evolution to this day; a computer program written to recreate the phrase METHINKS IT IS LIKE A WEASEL from *Hamlet*; and the author's goal – to distinguish between the concepts of single-step selection and cumulative selection. With the former, "the entities selected or sorted . . . are sorted once and for all" (1986/2015: 64). At Dawkins's invitation, consider the aforementioned hemoglobin, which is made of four entwined chains of 146 amino acids each. The likelihood of getting a single thread of hemoglobin molecule to come together by chance, given that there are 20 possible amino acids, is one in $20 \times 20 \times 20$ and so on, with 146 20s total (1986/2015: 63–64). However, with cumulative selection, "The entities are subjected to selection or sorting over many 'generations' in succession. The end-product of one generation of

---

[32] The Central Dogma is no longer considered inviolate, but it is usually the case.

selection is the starting point for the next generation of selection, and so on for many generations" (1986/2015: 65). Dawkins's program is a model of cumulative selection.

Dawkins starts his explanation of the program's specifics with a scene of writing from one variant of the form of the Infinite Monkey Theorem: a single monkey, infinite time, and, per usual, a typewriter and the assumption that nonhuman primates don't prefer one key over another. Let's lighten this monkey's load, Dawkins offers, with a special typewriter that has only capital letters and a space bar. The scientist's first gesture is to use his 11-month-old daughter as a "randomizing device" "step[ping] into the role of monkey typist." The first two lines of her contribution are the following:

UMMK JK CDZZ F ZD DSDSKSM
S SS FMCV PU I DDRGKDXRRDO

Failure. He puts down the baby. Calculating the chance of getting METHINKS IT IS LIKE A WEASEL in the same manner as he calculates the likelihood of getting one strand of a hemoglobin molecule, Dawkins comes to the number of approximately "1 in 10,000 million million million million million" (1986/2015: 66–67). Oof. The biologist then takes a new approach – cumulative selection. He writes a program in BASIC "to simulate a randomly typing baby or monkey" by selecting a sequence of 28 characters (the number of letters and spaces in the phrase from *Hamlet*). This is what it comes up with (and yes, the program is an it, the monkey is identified as a he, and the baby a she): "WDLMNLT DTJBKWIRZEZLMQCO P." Dawkins had already left for lunch.

The program does the work on its own. "It now 'breeds from' this random phrase. It duplicates it repeatedly, but with a certain chance of random error – 'mutation' – in the copying." The program selects whatever is closest to METHINKS IT IS LIKE A WEASEL. Repeat. Repeat. Repeat. Repeat. Repeat. Repeat. Repeat. Repeat. Repeat. In ten generations, we have "MDLDMNLS ITJISWHRZREZ MECS P." 20: "MELDINLS IT ISWPRKE Z WECSEL." 40: "METHINKS IT IS LIKE I WEASEL." Target at 43. Dawkins tries again, reaching full weasel in 64 generations. Again, and it takes only 41 (1986/2015: 68–70).

When Dawkins is developing his Weasel program, Richard Hardison is writing a similar *Hamlet* program with the goal text of TOBEORNOTTOBE. Both are unaware of each other's efforts but have a shared aim: challenging creationism in all its guises. Hardison's code operates on the same principle as Dawkins's, but requires more breeding. The former does some math and figures it would take his program 338 generations; with 1000 tries, it took on average 332.2. As he explains in his book *Upon the Shoulders of Giants*, "Extending this computer program so that it would construct the entire play would be a task of Herculean proportions, but if this were done, the actual writing of the play would require only about four and one half days" on his scrawny 80s desktop (Hardison, 1985: 125).

Here are the first lines of Hardison's code as printed in Appendix E of *Upon the Shoulders of Giants*, immediately after a lengthy footnoted complaint about astrology:

10 *REM 1984 R.HARDISON*
11 *PRINT "RANDOMIZING ALPHABET"*
12 *PRINT "WRITE HAMLET, KEEPING"*

13 *PRINT "SUCCESSES."* (1985: 345)

In BASIC, PRINT "does not literally 'print' anything in the way the word normally is used to indicate reproduction by marking a medium, as with paper and ink – instead, it displays" (Montfort et al., 2014: 11). The command is a vestige of the context of the language's original development. BASIC, or, Beginner's All-Purpose Symbolic Instruction Code (the language used to program Tognazzini's text game and Dawkins's, Hardison's, and Bennett's work), was created by Dartmouth math professors in 1964 for users working on "essentially glorified typewriters," screenless Teletype machines that printed on paper at the speed of 10 characters per second (McCracken: 2014).[33] Bennett's 1976 textbook on BASIC gives the same printing speed for the AR-33 Teletype as its 1964 forebears (Bennett, 1976: 107).

---

[33] Although BASIC was essential to the commodification of the personal computer and the accessibility of computing outside of industry and high-level research, some resented its minimalism and ease of use (McCracken, 2014).

We might ask, at this point, why is it Shakespeare in Dawkins's and Hardison's toy machines of evolution? Let's hear Dawkins's answer. In an email exchange included in Michael Shermer's "To Be or Not To Be a Weasel: Hamlet, Intelligent Design, and How Evolution Works," Dawkins explains that "those pesky monkeys have always typed Shakespeare" (2004: 16). Of course, we already know this not to be true. "Shakespeare colonized the metaphor," as Galey puts it, even weaseling himself retroactively into Borel's original formulation, made 17 years before Shakespeare would actually be mentioned in the same breath as typewriters and monkeys (Galey, 2014: 6; Hattenbach and Glucoft, 2015: 33). Dawkins continues, "Hamlet is his most famous play. To Be or Not to Be is the most famous passage from that play. I would probably have chosen it myself, except that I thought the dialogue between Hamlet and Polonius on chance resemblances in clouds would make a neat intro … " (Shermer, 2004: 16).

A more interesting question is this: what is Shakespeare doing for skeptics and believers? More interesting yet, at least to me: *what are the "Shakesperotics" of the code and the discourse that surrounds it?*

No *stable* function of Shakespeare will emerge as my argument proceeds. He is more human than human, but so human he is nonhuman; he is proof of the existence of divine agency and the lack thereof; his words are data and his words are genius and his words are treated as data but should never be because they are genius. What will hopefully become clear is that reanimating Shakespeare in this context is a way of tracing the relations between *Homo sapiens* and nonhuman intelligence, whether organic, sacred, and/or machinic. The computational recreation of Shakespeare's words becomes a measurement of what is lost or gained by what media theorist Vilém Flusser calls "another writing" and I call nonhuman writing (2011: 55). It is through the often playful appropriation of Shakespeare's texts that the metaphysics of writing as non/human can come to the often anxious and uncomfortable fore.

Even more remarkable, an examination of design theory's relentlessly indignant response to Dawkins's program suggests not only that *writing is non/human*, but also, in the age of research on and with genetic molecules, that *the non/human might have been relegated to mere word strings*. Put differently, the digitization, manipulation, and recreation of Shakespeare's texts are believed to be of a piece with the alleged desecration of the organism by molecular biology. The Infinite Monkey Theorem becomes, for some ID adherents, an accurate diagram of the violence of computation when applied to literature and to biological life, itself. Here, Shakespeare is a gauge that registers the injurious effects of informatization on our bodies and other sacred texts. And yet, for other design theorists, their field – which is focused on identifying patterns that index the action of an intelligent agent – is a heterodox branch of information theory, one that frequently relies on Shakespeare's sonnets and strings of DNA nucleotides to explain its key terms. Here, Shakespeare is a mechanism that can neutralize the threat posed by information so it can be used to legitimate design theory as real information science and allegedly prove the existence of a transcendental creator. When considered across this sometimes contradictory discourse, Shakespeare's oeuvre, frequently employed to demonstrate the value of patterns to literary analysis, is both an ideal collection of textual patterns always already informatized and a body whose organic wholeness succeeds or fails at overcoming the programming of human faculties.

2.2 Skeptics Read the Book of Life

Hardison's and Dawkins's BASIC programs were written to address a single aspect of arguments against evolution: the belief that Darwinism means a purely random concatenation of single-step selections that is, do the math (as Dawkins did with hemoglobin), well-nigh impossible. However, natural selection is actually cumulative, involving randomness *and* non-randomness. It is not random that some random mutations don't lead to viable organisms, some organisms survive to reproduce, and others are less suited to the exigencies of their environment. As Hardison puts it in relation to his own simulation with the target of TOBEORNOTTOBE, "nature keeps the successes and discards the failures. The gains are perpetuated, so to continue the typewriter analogy, when our simian friend happens upon a T, the letter is kept and he goes on randomly typing until he strikes an O, which in turn is retained. And so on" (Hardison, 1985: 124).

Cumulative selection is not ignored by design theorists William Dembski and Jonathan Wells. They dispatch with it quickly though a variant of the Infinite Monkey Theorem they attribute to Eugenie Scott, quoted at length in *The Design of Life*:

> [Suppose] you got a million monkeys sitting there typing on their machine. If you want to make this an analogy that makes sense from the standpoint of evolution, you've got a million technicians standing behind them with a very large vat of white out and every time the monkey types the wrong letter, you correct it. That's what natural selection basically does. It's not just the random production of variation. (qtd. in Dembski and Wells, 2008: 179)

Dembski and Wells remain entirely unconvinced. "The whole point of having monkeys at a typewriter is to account for the emergence of Shakespeare's works without the need to invoke an intelligence (like Shakespeare) that already knows Shakespeare's works . . . But that's not what is happening here. *Clearly, the only way to erase errors in the typing of Shakespeare's works is to know Shakespeare's works in the first place*" (2008: 180). Dembski and Wells attribute their response to a dedication to "scientific rigor," which mandates that they determine *who* is consulting the technicians on the right way to be Shakespeare. "Bottom line," they summarize in a strange formulation, "Monkeys cannot type Shakespeare apart from Shakespeare!" (2008: 180).

Dembski and Wells are arguing with Dawkins here, though they don't mention him by name in this particular discussion. They also leave out a key element of *The Blind Watchmaker*'s extended explanation of the goal of the Weasel program, which is only the first and deliberately most elementary of the two programs written for *The Blind Watchmaker*. Dawkins admits the following:

> Although the monkey/Shakespeare model is useful for explaining the distinction between single-step selection and cumulative selection, it is misleading in important ways. One of these is that, in each generation of selective 'breeding', the mutant 'progeny' phrases were judged according to

the criterion of resemblance to a distant ideal target, the phrase METHINKS IT IS LIKE A WEASEL. Life isn't like that. Evolution has no long-term goal. There is no long-distance target, no final perfection to serve as a criterion for selection, although human vanity cherishes the absurd notion that our species is the final goal of evolution. (Dawkins, 1986/2015: 72)

This problem with final perfection is commonly noted by critics of the Weasel program, even those sympathetic with Dawkins's struggle to clarify the mechanisms of evolution.

Holding the trouble with teleology closely in mind, Dawkins sets out to make a truer to life program he calls EVOLUTION. He rejects "letters and words" as "peculiarly human manifestations," making the purportedly less anthropocentric choice of creating software that draws pictures (Dawkins, 1986/2015: 72). And this time, he leaves the "misleading" telos behind, allowing drawings to emerge without judging them against the work of a distant and yet ever-present genius. The Weasel program is a preliminary step in an argument that breaks the phenomenon of natural selection into multiple parts explained sequentially in Chapter Three of *The Blind Watchmaker*. Subsequent sections of this argument are rarely mentioned by opponents.

One philosophical issue with teleology is the fact that, with these monkey simulators, there is an entity that *knows* that long-distance target in advance. This epistemological concern is addressed much earlier in the history of the Infinite Monkey Theorem in E. W. F. Tomlin's *Living and Knowing*, which provides a theologico-metaphysical account of biological life focusing on personhood. Tomlin prefaces his discussion of the "familiar conundrum" of monkeys typing Shakespeare with the assumption that while consciousness as such could not emerge from evolution, perhaps the nervous system could. "Now, according to the 'accident' theory, such a nervous system would enjoy the status of the 'Works of Shakespeare' produced fortuitously by monkeys pounding on typewriters for an infinite number of years" (Tomlin, 1955: 92). The difficulty here is that "the monkeys, engaged in their continuous typing, would no more be tempted to pause at the point at which they had completed the Works, than they would realize the point at which they had embarked upon them" (1955: 92–93). This situation would necessitate that "scholars" already know Shakespeare's oeuvre in order to bracket it off from the rest of the monkeys' output and presumably notify the typists that they have completed their mission (1955: 93). In other words, for the monkeys to know that they had reached their goal, they would need to rely on an external consciousness with foreknowledge of Shakespeare. Ultimately, Tomlin determines that "At every stage the salient features of consciousness – perception, memory, judgement, and over-sight – would need to be at work in order that the system should be what it is . . . The power enabling the nervous system to continue in being would be the activity presupposing its arrival" (1955: 93). Cognitive scientist Douglas Hofstadter makes an analogous but obverse argument in his critique of the claim that LLMs are actually conscious. While Tomlin's monkeys have no idea when they are succeeding, GPT-3 has no idea when it is failing. Indeed, "GPT-3 *has no idea that it has no idea* about what it is saying" (qtd. in Sejnowski, 2023: 336). "[T]he system just starts babbling randomly – but it has no sense that its random babbling is random babbling" (2023: 336–337). Of course, people who "probe it skeptically" like Hofstadter can alert the system that it is generating gibberish, and a change of tactic could possibly be made, as the imagined Shakespearean could intervene in the monkeys' effluvial flow (2023: 337).

Tomlin is working within a theistic framework, unlike Hofstadter. For the latter, the skeptical outsider who should notify the system of its mistakes is certainly human. For the former, whose story of monkeys, Shakespeare, and scholars is a parable of the emergence of human consciousness, the proposed expert is surely the Christian God (although Tomlin has not explicitly introduced the divine into this particular critique of natural selection). The suggestion that God does the duties of a cosmic Shakespeare scholar is a departure from the longstanding trend of associating God with Shakespeare, himself, and surely a remarkable appearance of Shakespeare in discourse outside of Shakespeare studies. Tomlin's bottom line: Monkeys can't type Shakespeare apart from supernatural Shakespeareans. Somebody must know what winning looks like.

The notion of final perfection is intimately tied to anthropomorphism, as accepting a process that has effects but lacks the action of an agent with intention has proven difficult for many. I might reframe this problem of agency as a problem of writing: Is there nonhuman writing? Or, according to Levi-Strauss, "Could there be something, as biologists claim, which resembles the structure of language but which involves neither consciousness nor subject?" (in Kay, 2000: 34). The challenge of imagining asubjective writing and finding appropriate language to describe it can be felt in discussions of computer programming, which needs humans but obviously involves the generative capabilities of the apparatus. As pearl-clutching computer scientist Edsger Dijkstra gasps in 1975, "the use of anthropomorphic terminology when dealing with computing systems is a symptom of professional immaturity" (Dijkstra, 1975/1982: 15).

In his own context, Dawkins negotiates the difficulties of the non/human by adopting a false anthropomorphism strategically and temporarily near the beginning of his chapter on cumulative selection. Darwin's relationship to anthropomorphism in *On the Origin of Species* follows a similar trajectory when tracked over several printings of the book, according to George Levine. "In the *Origin* he personifies natural selection as an intelligent being infinitely more perceptive than humanity and careful of the individual to which it 'tends,'" Levine writes. "But under the pressure of critics who saw 'natural selection' as an active force, actually producing variations, and personified as a living being, he became careful in later editions to remove the Romantic, loving figure, tending to its subjects, and to explain it in the driest language he could find" – brittle phrases approaching "the language of 'algorithm'" (Levine, 2006: 166).

In a fascinating discussion of metaphor, Levine connects this shift in Darwin's writing to two elements of his biography – the death of his beloved ten-year-old daughter, Annie, and a tragic admission in the scientist's *Autobiography*: "Now for many years I cannot endure to read a line of poetry: I have tried lately to read Shakespeare, and found it so intolerably dull that it nauseated me" (qtd. in Levine, 2006: 135). Is his physical revulsion a side effect of "aesthetic anesthesia," as it is often portrayed, in the face of the scientific truth of a mechanized world (Levine, 2006: 135)? Is this the gastrospiritual condition diagnosed by design theorists and creationists as the most problematic pathology of our time? Not necessarily, says Levine. Darwin's nausea can be understood as the intense feeling of a grieving man who turns away from Shakespeare to find poetry in the behavior of birds and the movement of plants toward the sun (Levine, 2006: 135–136). After Annie, there is no Shakespeare in Shakespeare (and younger Darwin passionately loved poetry), there is only Shakespeare in the theater of the natural world. And Darwin could find poetry in nature, could read it, actually, because he was originally "trained by literature," carried with him as dog-eared volumes, moist from tropical humidity, on ships around the world (Levine, 2006: 139).

As Levine articulates, returning to the problem of Darwin's figurative language (as I will return to this problem later in the section), "Stripping nature of the support of his marvelous metaphors, Darwin is forced to confront the meaninglessness and injustice of Annie's death. Only by removing 'natural selection' from the world of metaphor, which it inhabited in all the early versions of his theory, Darwin in effect gives up on poetry as well, and only then could he live with it" (Levine, 2006: 166). Annie died – on Shakespeare's birthday, no less – because animals die, and the beauty of her life is also the poetry of natural things, of the intelligent worms, of the finches. He cannot conceive of Annie's death as by design, and "If the death of neither man or gnat [or daughter] are designed," there is certainly "no good reason to believe that their *first* birth or production shd be necessarily designed" (qtd. in Levine, 2006: 164).

Darwin's occasional use of the language of agency is not lost on design theorists. Indeed, it is lovingly clenched as indicative of the untenability of evolutionary theory. *Of Pandas and People* reminds its high school readers that Darwin himself "ascribe[s] remarkable skill to natural selection." The textbook continues:

> Since Darwin's time, biological literature has honored nat-
> ural selection with metaphors of great artistry and skill,
> comparing it to a composer of music, a master of ceremo-
> nies, a poet, a sculptor, and "William Shakespeare." More
> recently, natural selection has become identified with the
> metaphor of the Blind Watchmaker, through Richard
> Dawkins' book so titled. (Davis and Kenyon, 1996: 67)

While the theory of natural selection ultimately says that what only looks like good design, and might be explained as such metaphorically, is really an unconscious process without telos, design theory embraces the simpler explanation – it is just good design by a supernatural designer. By this argument, nature, itself, shouldn't be considered truly creative, but both Shakespeare and God (or aliens) should. Darwinist metaphorical language points to a deeper truth, imply ID supporters.

However, fully reckoning with natural selection means situating the human within immanent natural but nonhuman and nonconscious processes of biological change affecting all organic life. This reorientation of the human is a key part of a larger metaphysical shift with consequences that can't be underestimated: specifically, the theory of natural selection "removed design and teleology from nature, replacing them with explanations in which causes always precede effects, and nothing but physical law guides the course of all systems, including biological ones" (Sakar, 2007: 14). Physical law and the natural world governed by it are worthy of wonder, but they are anthrodecentric. By attempting "to resuscitate design and teleology," ID proponents are reanimating a metaphysics in which humans are the ultimate goal of divine action, squandering the potential anthrodecentrism of the notion of a divinely authored universe (Sakar, 2007: 14).

Less obvious here is the formulation of writing in this debate. From its early-twentieth century inception, the Infinite Monkey Theorem has been a computational thought experiment, even without the use of computers, that imagines a scene of writing as technologically dependent, nonconscious, nonhuman, and yet also dependent on human authorship (Shakespeare). And what is the writing executed by the Weasel program and TOBEORNOTTOBE but technologically dependent, nonconscious, nonhuman and yet also dependent on human authorship through the human programmer as well as Shakespeare as the creator of "final perfection"? ID's argument that monkeys could only type Shakespeare if someone already familiar with Shakespeare's writing performed the function of error detection is another way of stating what Dawkins has already disclosed – that the operation of Shakespeare in this formulation makes the Weasel program *unlike* evolution, for evolution is writing which actually has no author, no target text in mind, and no (conscious) mind at all. Indeed, when considered not a story about the absence of God but a story about the generation of text, natural selection is a theory of nonconscious asubjective authorship that belongs in conversations about writing's ontology.

I can't leave metaphor aside. Not yet. In a compilation of reader responses to Dawkins's and Hardison's programs published in the magazine *Skeptic* in 2004, there is considerable discomfort with the primary metaphor of monkeys typing Shakespeare (even though the readership of the magazine must skew towards those who have sharpened their teeth against the influence of creationism in all its forms, including the creationist thinking lurking in theories of ID) (Shermer, 2004: 17–20). Indeed, one extended theme in the pages of *Skeptic* is the blasted trickiness of common metaphors in genetic science, an admonishment we have already heard from Kay in her book *Who Wrote the Book of Life?: A History of the Genetic Code.* Biologist William Stansfield focuses on the failure of the Shakespeare metaphor in a stand-alone rejoinder to Hardison's and Dawkins's code. Stansfield's opinion piece, titled "Hamlet Revisited: How Evolution Really Works" and also published in *Skeptic*, admits that "Metaphors can sometimes be very useful educational tools. However, I believe that the typing-monkeys metaphor generated by Hardison and Dawkins are so unlike biological realities and the way that natural selection operates that they will only tend to confuse students, rather than help them learn" (Stansfield, 2004: 18). Here, Stansfield severs the connection between a protein like hemoglobin and a line from Shakespeare:

> there currently are more than 100 amino acid substitutions known in the beta chains of normal adult human hemoglobin. Most of these variants produce a functional protein, so most people who carry them are usually unaware of it. By contrast, the full meaning (function) of the English phrase "tobeornottobe" makes no sense (is not fully functional) until all 13 letters are in their respective positions. (Stansfield, 2004: 17)

There is only one "tobeornottobe." Then there is the set of {everything that is not Shakespeare's most famous equivocation}. That is not how biology works.

    To be sure, if the genome can indeed be considered a language – an
uncanny language that can mysteriously exist outside and prior to human
discourse – then it generates sense quite differently than languages derived
from human consciousness. Following reader R. Reece in his letter from the
previous issue, Stansfield proposes that we temporarily run with the metaphor
and consider "Two be or knot too be" to be "close enough for evolutionary
forces to generate" (Stansfield, 2004: 16). However, this misspelling adds
three more letters to Hamlet's thirteen-letter phrase. Since DNA codes for
amino acids through groups of three nucleotide bases, analogized here as
letters, a change of three additional nucleotides in various places in the string
would cause a frameshift mutation, a particularly impactful problem "that
could render the protein useless if they occurred in the reactive site of the
chain or caused the chain to fold improperly. If the shifted reading frame
created a nonsense triplet, the length of the protein would prematurely stop
there and the truncated protein would probably not function" (Stansfield,
2004: 18). Twobeorknottoobe and tobeornottobe sound the same in the
context of live performance, but in the context of the genome, a shift
analogous to the former might catastrophically alter the meaning. Stansfield
takes issue with any rhetorical use of monkeys typing *Hamlet* in the context of
molecular biology, ending his essay with a dad joke: "'quit monkeying
around.' Just tell it like it is" (Stansfield, 2004: 18). No monkeys. No typewriters. And definitely no Shakespeare.

    Although I believe the Infinite Monkey Theorem has been adequately
deployed by Neo-Darwinists as an analogy for one concept in evolutionary
science, it suffers from a *formal problem* for proponents of evolution when
misrepresented as accountable for all aspects of natural selection. The
Theorem stages a scene of writing that both divides and fuses Shakespeare
as author from/to an assemblage of technology and nonhuman primates. In
other words, it is a strange obversion of Artaud-via-Derrida's *theological
stage* – in this case, both grammatological *and* governed by an absent and
transcendental authority (Derrida, 1978: 235). This unusual theological form
roughly coincides with a diagram that both separates and conjoins an extraterrestrial Intelligent Designer from/with "His" human and nonhuman
terrestrial creations. The congruity between Author and Designer in these
diagrams – especially relevant given the frequency with which ID is

explained through analogies to writing – produces a kind of formal sublime terror for design theorists that is the serious counterpart to the formal horror-comedy so brilliantly displayed in #infinitemonkeytheorem on TikTok. Shakespeare may not be God, but he performs a God-like function. The Christian God, only loosely veiled by the concept of Intelligent Designer, is the supernatural playwright of the whole wide world, and an attack on *Hamlet* is an attack on authorship is an attack on God's creation.

Relevant here is Flusser's *Does Writing Have a Future?*, which secures the ontology of writing within Biblical narratives of creation. Writing is an inscription or incision: the Latin *scribere* means "to scratch," while the Greek word *graphein* means "to dig." Writing is, at its heart, a kind of scratching and digging in clay, apparent in the story that "God made his own image in clay (Hebrew: *adamah*), infused the clay with his own breath, and so created a human being (Hebrew: *adam*)." Flusser insists that "the invention of writing can be recognized in this myth. The Mesopotamian clay in the myth is shaped into a tablet, which is engraved with the holy wedge-shaped stylus, and so the first inscription (human being) was created" (2011: 11–12). Adam is thus the writing of God. Per Flusser's larger concerns in a book that serves as a conflicted elegy for writing as we have come to know it for so long, computer programming is "another writing," although it shares with some conventional writing an orientation towards technological action (2011: 55). Indeed, Flusser claims that "people have been programming since writing was invented – before there were any apparatuses. For one wrote to human beings as though they were apparatuses." Flusser continues:

> these instructions constitute a prominent thread in the advancing discursive mesh we call Western literature. Using this thread to guide us in a survey of Western history, the development can be represented as follows: at the beginning, since the Stele of Hammurabi, these instructions were called "commandments"; then, with the Twelve Tablets, they became "laws," which later branched out into decrees, regulations, and other forms of instruction; during the Industrial Revolution, instructions were added that pertained to people's behavior toward machines, or "user's manuals"; until finally,

since the informatic revolutions, the program discussed earlier – namely, instructions to machines – completed this
development. Programs are not only a completely new
way of writing, they are also the culmination of a pattern
established when writing began. (2011: 56)

Since surely the Ten Commandments would be included in this history, we
might call computers scriptural technologies – akin to whatever scratched
lines in moist clay and incised basalt, to the clay and basalt, akin to the finger
of God that dug commands into stone slabs, to all the fingers and the breath
of God, to Moses's chisel, and to Moses, himself, transformed into a writing
machine when God orders him to remake the Tablets of the Law, flung and
shattered at the foot of the mount.

[*He writes.*] (Shakespeare)

2.3 No Nausea in the Theater of the Fields

History has proven that the likening of Shakespeare to the Christian God is not
heresy, given the frequency with which Shakespearean genius has been understood as divine, as discussed in Section 1. The most developed argument for
Shakespeare's God-like status in the context of design theory – and, for me, the
most interesting appearance of the Infinite Monkey Theorem – is in Benjamin
Wiker and Jonathan Witt's *A Meaningful World: How the Arts and Sciences
Reveal the Genius of Nature*, which puts Shakespeare at the center of its polemic
against Dawkins, (Neo-)Darwinism at large, and scientific materialism most
generally. The book's primary claim regarding Shakespeare is that his works
can teach us to identify genius in an author's creation, that these very attributes
can be found in nature (observable in "the chemical makeup of our world"), and
that the presence of these attributes necessarily indexes an "Author of the
Cosmos" (2006: 180, 55). Through extended readings of *Hamlet* and *The
Tempest*, Wiker and Witt isolate "criteria of genius" in a work of art that can
also be applied outside of literary creation: namely, "depth," "harmony,"
"elegance," and (in a term that could have come from Agamben's discussion
of the anthropogenic machine), "anthropic clarity," which "impress[es] on the
human viewer as much of the play's richness as possible and, indeed, teach[es]

him about the depths and contours of his own human nature" (2006: 75–80). Throughout the book, the authors compare the alleged deposition of God by science to various critiques of Shakespeare and his work. Wiker and Witt take potshots at psychoanalysis, deconstruction, postmodernism, Marxism, and gender studies as all reducible to the apocalyptic nihilism induced by science's unwavering insistence on material causes. Indeed, "The materialist attack on the Author of nature led to a loss of confidence in the literary author as source to stabilize meaning," they write, tracing a causal relationship between Darwin's theory of natural selection and Roland Barthes's "Death of the Author" (2006: 40). Darwinists and Freudians (and, we presume, Barthesians), say Wiker and Witt, "tried to grind Shakespeare into dust" (2006: 46). And why? "The most obvious reason is that Shakespeare was too traditional, too much the dead white Christian male, too much the theist. More subtly (and this motivation need not be a conscious one in every case), Shakespeare's very art is a powerful argument against the notion that we are but the accidental outcome of a mindless material mechanism" (2006: 48). The authors use their impassioned dismissal of the possibility of monkeys typing the Bard's work to reanimate a Shakespeare allegedly murdered and then incinerated by materialists, monkey lovers, post-structuralists, and (implicitly), computation, itself.

Wiker and Witt's extended critique of Dawkins's monkey/Shakespeare model in their chapter "*Hamlet* and the Search for Meaning," worth reading closely for the explicitness of its handling of the anthropogenic machine, is an exegesis of the play that is also a theory of dramatic literature and a condemnation of genetic science. Opening with the confident assertion that an exploration of *Hamlet* proves that "efforts to reduce Shakespeare's gifts to blind material causes" can only fail, the authors quickly turn to the performance at the Paington Zoo I describe in Section 1. The dramatic failure of Elmo, Gum, Heather, Holly, Mistletoe, and Rowan to reproduce Shakespeare's oeuvre is presented as proof of "the squishy empirical foundations of the Darwinists' typing monkeys claim," with the monkey shit on the keyboard forming an apt image of the profanation of God by science (2006: 32). This scatological scene of writing sets the stage for the authors' consideration of METHINKS IT IS LIKE A WEASEL as not rigorous intellectual inquiry, but "an ingenious and meticulously structured piece of rhetoric" that uses the immediate context of the line – Hamlet and

Polonius discussing figures they see in the clouds – as a subtle burn against Christianity for its hazy, ungrounded beliefs (2006: 36).

Dawkins, though, is ultimately a poor reader of Shakespeare. Wiker and Witt set him straight with a restorative summary of the plot of the play and a description of Polonius as a bullshitter who does not actually see the shapes of animals in the sky, but only tells Hamlet what he thinks the prince wants to hear. Dawkins's dislocation of the phrase from the play at large is even worse than his program's inadequacy as a simulation of evolution. By this argument, Dawkins can use the phrase "Methinks it is like a weasel" to contend that the world is meaningless (allegedly) because he has forcibly pried the line from its rightful place in the very textual environment that gives it meaning. "Dawkins and other Darwinists treat biological traits and lines of genetic information in the same misguided way – as 'phrases' that can exist somehow apart from the real, living dramatic unity of biological organisms" (2006: 37). This is a crisis in science, assert Wiker and Witt, and it is a crisis in literary studies. "In each case the critic analyzes the work narrowly, ignoring the larger context, be it ecological, aesthetic or otherwise" (2006: 56). Science disregards the organism, and literary studies, naively following twentieth century philosophy, shuns "the notion of organic wholes" (2006: 79). In other words, Wiker and Witt advocate for "the theological system" Gilles Deleuze and Félix Guattari critique with the concept of the Body without Organs (BwO), borrowed from Artaud: "*The judgment of God*, the system of the judgment of God, the theological system, is precisely the operation of He who makes an organism, an organization of organs called the organism, because He cannot bear the BwO ... " (1987: 158–159). Wiker and Witt understand this system as fundamentally *dramaturgical*, with Shakespeare's plays as both example and model.

The authors also echo an early critique of the digital humanities recounted in the very first issue of *Computers and the Humanities* (September 1966): humanities researchers who use computational analysis are often "victims of a fallacy by which they reduce wholes to discrete parts that are disconnected from the value or nature of the whole" (Leed, 1966: 13). Remarkably, the next chapter of *A Meaningful World* explicitly connects the severing of the part from the whole to a failure to see Shakespeare's plays *in performance*. "[I]t's possible to believe reductionist treatments of Shakespeare if all one has read is the reductionist treatments themselves," the authors complain, "avoiding the very theater within which we might be delivered from such misreading. In short, we need to *experience* Shakespeare's genius." Similarly, they insist, "It is easy to believe the reduction of butterflies to atoms and energy if we have never attended to a butterfly in the theater of the fields" (2006: 62–63). Wiker and Witt's implicit theory of dramatic literature super/naturalizes both live performance and dramaturgical form as complete bodies granting us access to a grand textual ecology of human and divine genius – without which the world is tragically without meaning, a stream of piss poor Ss.

The Weasel program fails at proving the world is meaningless, though, because it is not part of an argument about the meaninglessness of the world. In fact, Dawkins points out that the assumption that natural selection is random and meaningless is a common misunderstanding (although certainly meaning as design theorists intend it is not his concern, and he is fond of pointing at the fundamental indifference of nature to human-centered matters) (1986/2015: 54). More interesting to me than Wiker and Witt's mischaracterization of Dawkins's work is their integration of Shakespeare and the Infinite Monkey Theorem within their emergent critique of what we might call, following Eugene Thacker, *biomedia*. "Biomedia are novel configurations of biologies and technologies" that are shaped "by a single assumption" – "that there exists some fundamental equivalency between genetic 'codes' and computer 'codes,' or between the biological and digital domains, such that they can be rendered interchangeable in terms of materials and functions" (2004: 5, 6). Through practices like bioinformatics and biocomputation, biomedia have "the ability to isolate and abstract certain types of essential data, or patterns of relationships, which are independent of and mobile across varying media, or material substrates" (2004: 28). Thacker details the historical development and underlying logic of biology as "a science of informatics" based not on the augmentation of the body or even the digitization of life, but on the belief that DNA is *always already computational* (2004: 28).

Thacker's goals are clearly very different than those of Wiker and Witt, with his bio-ethical stance at odds with the theistic moralizing of *A Meaningful World*. That said, the former's explanation of changes wrought to the idea and praxis of the body through biomedia has something in common with Wiker and Witt's articulation of the problem with Dawkins's approach to Shakespeare and the science of DNA:

> It is all too common, unfortunately, to believe that any living thing can be reduced to its DNA, and that its DNA can then be reduced to strings of the paired nucleic "letters" A, G, C and T (adenine, guanine, cytosine, thymine) and that these letters can be reduced to their elemental constituent chemical letters, N, H, O and C (nitrogen, hydrogen, oxygen, carbon). Indeed, as we know from Dawkins's larger corpus, such a belief is at the foundation of his use of Hamlet. On this view, every living thing is just a string of chemical letters. But that is a fundamental error ... The play isn't essentially a string of letters or even a string of five acts. Its meaning is manifested from both the whole and its milieu. The error concerning DNA consists in believing that we can isolate the functional entity (the sentences or DNA) apart from that in which and by which it has function ... The cell is not, contrary to common presentation, merely a biological after-thought, a convenient container in which to keep DNA; rather the cell is the integrated complex whole within which DNA as DNA can function ... (2006: 43)

Earlier in the book, Wiker and Witt analogize "the exquisite architecture of the cell that makes possible the work of DNA" to the pages of a book, "pages made of the appropriate material, properly ordered and bound" (2006: 20) (As Galey writes of *Hamlet*, "faith in the text begins with the form of the book" [Galey, 2012: 89]). Thacker, Wiker, and Witt are all responding to a general situation of biomediation "predicated on the ability to separate patterns of relationships from material substrates," which are then typically treated as, however essential, only "a vehicle for data" (Thacker, 2004: 28).[34]

---

[34] It is important to note that Thacker does not see biomedia as a posthumanist dematerialization of the body, because the information still needs the platform (Thacker: 2004, 28).

Wiker and Witt's challenge to these pervasive conditions of biomediation through their discussion of the purported failure of the Infinite Monkey Theorem is prescient considering a recent use of the Theorem, in an online hog industry journal, to illustrate a particular system of bioengineering using CRISPR genome editing. After a drawing of a typing monkey in formalwear being consulted by an anthropomorphized CAS9 protein hovering over its shoulder, the author explains, "Now imagine that we can tell the monkey to rewrite just a specific page in Shakespeare's Macbeth. Limited to just this narrow window, the monkey will type out every possible variation of the page's text much, much faster. This is what EvolvR lets scientists do" (Alumbaugh, 2018). Surely, this is version 2.0 of Wiker and Witt's cut-paste bio-literary nightmare.

What I find most engaging about *A Meaningful World* is the authors' obsessive positioning of Shakespeare scholarship at the very center of their diagnosis of a science-induced gastrospiritual disorder. For Wiker and Witt, the alleged refusal of criticism to address his plays as complex organic wholes crafted by an author with superior "ordering powers" perpetuates the unraveling of Shakespearean genius begun by Darwin in the nineteenth century and continued by his twentieth and twenty-first century familiars like Dawkins (Wiker and Witt, 2006: 245). "The result is that the commonsense understanding of Shakespeare as a unified, thinking, acting, creative human being who wrote extraordinary dramas about other unified, thinking, acting human beings is itself destroyed" (2006: 245). Additionally, they maintain, Darwin's idea of natural selection has led to the rejection of authorial intention as the primary driver of literary criticism, which, in turn, has almost fatally compromised our ability to see "something like the fingerprints of an Author" in the elegantly ordered cosmos (2006: 19). Although Wiker and Witt do not explicitly blame computation, their use of Dawkins's Weasel program as a rhetorical touchstone invites an understanding of the perceived assault on Shakespeare as at least partially effected by the stringification of *Hamlet* and of biological life (with string, as the authors well know, denoting a sequence of characters in computer programming).

In this context, the Theorem's computational nature functions in the book as an illustration of the replacement of traditional authorship, but by what? A kind of writing that is only the subjectless assembly of letters generated by bioinformatic bodies making shitty, herky-jerky contact with a technological apparatus. God is dead, says philosophy, and so is the organism. Shakespeare can no longer be imagined composing his plays, quill paused, mind occupied by the elegant harmonies of *Homo sapiens*'s superior airs. Monkeys could bash a keyboard with rocks and still be called typists, but once programmed computationally, even our lithics are ground to dust. This is the tragedy of the "postvital body." As Richard Doyle explains in his critique of biomolecular discourse, the postvital body is unlike "the modern body of the organism," with the latter's "deep unity at work in its depths." Instead, it is "a body in which the distinct, modern categories of surface and depth, being and living, implode into the new density of coding" (Doyle, 1997: 13). The diminishment of Shakespeare and his work has the same desperate trajectory, for Wiker and Witt – a loss of organic unity and depth, a loss of being and living, an implosion into infinite code. Thus, the pulverization of Shakespeare is a stand-in not only for the death of God and death of the author, but the derogation of the human organism as a meaningful whole, the dismissal of the cell, and the reduction of genetic molecules to a letter-based code. The duty of the theist is to restore functional relationships between parts and wholes by analyzing the dramaturgy of God's creation performed in the theater of the fields.

While *A Meaningful World* contains an implicit critique of bioinformatics as violently anti-dramaturgical, design theory as a whole generally embraces the language of computation (or what passes as such). This is unsurprising, considering the charge of the primary research body of ID, the Discovery Institute, to reveal "a universe brimming with information and intelligent design."[35] In fact, an orientation towards a kind of information can be seen at the discourse's very beginnings. Take *Of Pandas and People*, which reminds its high school readers to "Recall that the DNA is a molecular message. A mutation is a random change in the message, akin to a typing error. Typing errors rarely improve the quality of a written message; if too many occur, they may even destroy the information contained in it" (Davis and Kenyon, 1996: 12). Dembski, whose concept of

---

[35] www.discovery.org/about/.

Complex Specified Information I deal with in Section 1, defines ID as "a theory for detecting and measuring information, explaining its origin, and tracing its flow" (in strategic contradistinction to the Flood geology of creationism, to be sure) (Dembski, 1998). Indeed, despite what I (and the courts) perceive as the obvious continuities with classic creationism, I would characterize most design theory as fusing the older paradigm of the organism with aspects of the new paradigm of postvitality.

Indicative of this line of thought is the following quotation from an essay on exploregod.com, a website that hybridizes design theory with a revamped creationism's Biblical rhetoric:

> First, biology becomes the study of complicated and beauti-
> ful things that, at their very core, operate on the basis of
> a digital code. Second, this genetic code is revealed as
> a language that communicates within the cell, through
> proteins, and between cells. Third, our only other exposure
> to informational codes or language is humans and the
> machines we design. Informational codes require prepro-
> gramming. In simpler terms, informational codes require
> a mind to create them, an intelligence that designs them …
> The language of DNA seems to be speaking of such
> a designer, a designer consistent with the God of the
> Bible. (Bohlin, n.d.)

Here, the author – with a different point of view than that of Wiker and Witt – reminds us that DNA is always already language and code, and, for proponents of common sense (and for those with an appreciation of aesthetics), such text must necessitate an author. Although media studies scholar Joanna Zylinska does not come to the same conclusion, relevant here is her insistence on *Homo sapiens*'s originary technicity on the grounds of the ontologically computational nature of DNA: "Humans' everyday functioning also depends on the execution of a programme: a sequence of possibilities enabled by various couplings of adenine, cytosine, guanine, and thymine, i.e. DNA." (Zylinska, 2020: 53). Dawkins would agree with Zylinska. "The machine code of the genes is uncannily computerlike.

Apart from differences in jargon, the pages of a molecular biology journal might be interchanged with those of a computer-engineering journal. Among other consequences, this digital revolution at the very core of life has dealt the final, killing bow to vitalism – the belief that living material is deeply distinct from nonliving material" (1995: 20). Code-lovers like Bohlin render the line between the living and nonliving ambiguous, while simultaneously shifting vitalist attention to the life of the God who wrote the sacred digital code.

Formal horror, this time based not on zeros and ones or the coupling of bases, but on the tyranny of the future over a purported origin: Expecting scientific advance to displace the need for a Creator is like getting two-thirds of the way through Hamlet and expecting the ending of the play to displace the need for Shakespeare (Ortlund, n.d.). A failed dramaturgy. My response: HAMLET THE DANE PRINCE AND MAGGOT'S FODDER STUMBLING FROM HOLE TO HOLE TOWARDS THE FINAL HOLE (Müller, 1980: 146).

For Wiker and Witt, it is we who have stumbled. We have become disoriented in relation to our bodies, our theater, and our world. Their prescription is for renewed attention to our origin in Biblical creation that is also a revitalized theater criticism as well as a rejuvenated biology. While this isn't what the STEM to STEAM movement has in mind, it does offer a remarkable and, at times, bizarre case for the utility of (a certain approach to) studying Shakespeare for nothing less than a syncretic reorganization of our techno-scientific and theological commitments. More modestly, their call for a sensitivity to the so-called glorious wholeness of plays and organisms attempts to disinter Shakespeare from his final hole, reassemble his rended parts, and *reanimate* him – in a process that aligns, to some extent, with Shakespeare reanimations we have already encountered. While Wiker and Witt would abhor this comparison, their idea of a unique authorial signature – the "signature of genius in nature" as well as in *Hamlet*, underscored throughout *A Meaningful World* – is not entirely unlike the notion of authorial signature in computational stylistics and the kinds of textual patterns exploited by Shakespeare bots (2006: 28). That said, Wiker and Witt obviously advocate for a return to a kind of humanism that no longer holds. Indeed, such humanism was inoperative even in the time of the very author whose intentions allow us to hear the organic harmonies of sacred composition. Renaissance reading, writing, and publishing practices were piecemeal and composite, as Peter Stallybrass reminds us, resisting the unity and homogeneity that Wiker and Witt demand (Stallybrass, 2007: 1581).

2.4 The Deep-Sea Octopus Who Learned to Make Meaningful Tapping

How has the Infinite Monkey Theorem "cast a kind of malignant charm" for so damn long (Wiker and Witt, 2006: 30)? How has a subsequent computer simulation written in BASIC and described in a book mightily provoked us for nearly 40 years? How does the program's so-called "combinatorial cataclysm" continue to be felt with calamitous force (Holloway, 2022)? How has all of this managed to lodge so tightly in theistic craws?

Importantly, although Dawkins's (and Hardison's) monkey programs were written immediately prior to the founding of the ID Movement, the argument from design has been well known since William Paley's *Natural Theology, or Evidence of the Existence and Attributes of the Deity, Collected from the Appearances of Nature* (1802), even if intelligence had yet to emerge as a primary concept driving Christian theological research on biology. Dawkins's bestselling *The Blind Watchmaker* was written *as if* in direct response to ID avant la lettre, and consequently continues to be condemned publicly on blogs and the pages of ID books to this day. Shakespeare is key to METHINKS IT IS LIKE A WEASEL's ongoing hold over a debate that has largely forgotten the other programs detailed in *The Blind Watchmaker*. The Bard's god-like status – his problematic position at the apex of the English-language canon as traditionally conceived; his longstanding association with genius as divine force; the credit the god incarnate has received for inventing the human as we understand it; the belief that he and the Christian God share fallen fortunes at the hands of Darwin; and the perceived consonance between his dramaturgy and that performed in the theater of the fields – is the largest contributor to the considerable rhetorical power of Dawkins's monkey/Shakespeare model. Indeed, the program's unrelenting ability to aggravate professional design theorists and social media commentators alike is in large part due to Dawkins's choice to work with Shakespeare's writing.

Moreover, continuing interest in Dawkins's appropriation of Shakespeare has likely been energized by the contemporary currency of the Infinite Monkey Theorem as an analogy for the diminishment of writing's humanity by technology. As I have already detailed, the Theorem frequently comes up, either explicitly or as the obvious inspiration behind an accompanying illustration, in discussions of the danger of ChatGPT and other bots run by LLMs. Take the banner accompanying the article "ChatGPT: Educators Hold Emergency Meetings as AI Disrupts Schools and Universities Across Australia," which references the Theorem in the body of the text (Hiatt, 2023). At the top of the web page is a glossy simian robot with exposed cables sitting in front of a laptop and staring vacuously at the superimposed logo for OpenAI. The monkey – it's really an ape, but we'll go with presumed intention – wears headphones; its forearms and hands aren't visible (Hiatt, 2023). Is it even writing? The longer I gaze at this techno-monkey the more confused I become. Is it the author of the students' homework, or does the monkey stand for the lazy 9th grader who can sit Google-eyed listening to hot trax while ChatGPT does all the work? "To most, ChatGPT is just the typewriters. And WE are the stupid monkeys" (Yu, 2023).

Such use of the Infinite Monkey Theorem has easily gained momentum in the past couple of years because of a prior association between monkeys failing to type Shakespeare's work and the valueless gibberish of netizens, mentioned in the previous section. As tweeted by qikipedia, "We've all heard that a million monkeys banging on a million typewriters will eventually reproduce the entire works of Shakespeare. Now, thanks to the Internet, we know this is not true. ROBERT WILENSKY." "Well, if he is an indicator of the people working on AI, then we are all in trouble," TheFLASH replies. *Have they read Shakespeare?/We're going bananas/It was only ever a metaphor, you know./I beg to differ.*[36] As AI expert Lance Eliot explains, "The joke is a putdown on how the Internet with all its frothing and spewing postings is nary rising to the level of producing Shakespeare" (Eliot, 2023).

Eliot begrudgingly accepts the joke as a critique of the Internet, although exaggerated. However, he vehemently contests the applicability of the Infinite Monkey Theorem to Generative AI like ChatGPT. While he

---

[36] twitter.com/qikipedia/status/1410576420363857926?lang=en.

acknowledges that a "somewhat unspoken underlying element is that monkeys are being used in this case because we consider them to be relatively unthinking. They do not know how to read or write. They are not able to exhibit intelligence in the same manner that we associate intelligence with human capacities," he maintains that monkeys *are* thinking creatures, however "limited." Generative AI does not think, or even "think," he insists; it is not sentient, despite occasional claims to the contrary. It is "a computer-based statistical mimicry" that "makes use of a complex mathematical and computational formulation that has been set up by examining patterns in written words and stories across the web" (Eliot, 2023).

And yet, the Infinite Monkey Theorem seems to many to be an appropriate metaphor for LLMs, a metaphor that reinforces the similarity of chatbots to nonhuman animals. Other charismatic animal species with impressive capacities are points of reference for the capabilities and deficiencies of LLMs. Monkeys join a menagerie in the literature that includes numerous "stochastic parrots," a "talking dog," and a "hyperintelligent deep-sea octopus," all of which can imitate human communication in the presented scenarios but don't, according to the assumption, understand it (Bender et al., 2021; Sejnowski, 2023: 309–310; Weil, 2023). Despite Eliot's protestations, the typing monkey has the perfect combination of presumed mechanistic randomness and sophisticated primate intelligence to make it a popular illustration of AI that writes. The likening of a LLM to a nonhuman animal, however hyperintelligent, reinforces the superiority of humans; at the same time, it suggests that there could be something computational about the intelligence of the natural world. This un/natural intelligence not only imitates us so successfully but also might transform us into vacant eyed simians jacked into a machine, missing the essential humanity that only doing homework on Shakespeare can give us.

As a conclusion to this section, it is worthwhile to track the idea of the artificiality of intelligence across the work of the two main monkey programmers discussed thus far, Bennett and Dawkins (Hardison doesn't address it in his brief explanation of TOBEORNOTTOBE). Let's begin with the very first computational instantiations of the Infinite Monkey Theorem, Bennett's monkey Shakespeare programs from 1976. While these programs were not successful at reproducing *Hamlet*, Bennett offers his methodology as a form of speculative thought to help us consider the relationship between the statistical properties of language and an author's characteristic voice and style. His method for recreating Shakespearean language is different from that of Dawkins and Hardison. As I explain earlier, Bennet starts by gathering first-, second-, third-, and fourth-order correlation data that establish the frequency of letters within particular texts. Correlation matrices are tables for such data, which Bennett chooses to display using the size and brightness of a blob to indicate a letter combination's relative occurrence, with the common pairing of T and H in Act III of *Hamlet*, for example, appearing larger and more prominent. Anticipating LLMs as well as the animal metaphors used in discussing these models, Bennett proposes with confidence that "a monkey program using fourth- or fifth-order correlation matrices loaded with clichés would be indistinguishable from the average political speech" (Bennett, 1977: 702). More speculatively, he offers that "the differences between Beethoven and Hummel [might] have been just one higher dimension in a matrix" (Bennett, 1972: 702). Presumably as an explanation of the article's tagline – "The great works of literature and art are not merely rare statistical fluctuations, but are they simply the products of correlation matrices?" – he suggests the following (1977: 694):

> One common characteristic of many outstanding creative geniuses is an early period of intense concentration on previous work in their field – frequently to the exclusion of most other activity. It could be argued that the main function of this period in the life of the artist is to select and store the requisite high-order correlation data and that the rest of the problem is just random choice with a weighting procedure of the type outlined above. (1977: 702)

Genius might very well be as programmed as software. How artificial is human intelligence? Perhaps, very. Perhaps there is something computational at the center of Shakespeare and other of our most creative minds. The *New York Times* broadens Bennett's basic position on genius to apply to the human language faculty most generally in their report on his research (Rensberger, 1979). "The experiments have prompted speculation about the extent to which the human mind may employ similar rules as part of its neurological programming for language," Rensberger writes, reminding us of the desire for a general theory of computation that drove early research on AI, including that of Minsky and Papert (Minsky and Papert, 2017: 1; Rensberger, 1979).

And where is intelligence in Dawkins's work? *The Blind Watchmaker* says little about it directly. Dawkins does offer a wonderfully unstable claim that "Cumulative selection, whether artificial selection as in the computer model or natural selection out there in the real world, is an efficient searching procedure, and its consequences look very like creative intelligence" (Dawkins, 1986/2015: 93). Presumably, given a refrain throughout his publications, he means that cumulative selection *only appears to be* creative intelligence, an illusion that fools theists of all kinds. By the end of the same paragraph, Dawkins admits that "Effective searching procedures become, when the search-space is *sufficiently* large, indistinguishable from true creativity," eroding the very confidence that would neatly discriminate between true creative intelligence on the one hand and the generativity of nature and computation the other (Dawkins, 1986/2015: 94). Tellingly, Dawkins puts cumulative selection in simulations and in the theater of the fields *on the same hand*, not only justifying his use of programming to model natural processes, but also implying that differences between "artificial" and "natural" intelligence might not matter all that much, especially at scale. Dawkins then returns to the second program of *The Blind Watchmaker*, EVOLUTION, insisting that it provides an "instructive bridge between human creative processes, such as planning a winning strategy at chess, and the evolutionary creativity of natural selection, the blind watchmaker" (Dawkins, 1986/2015: 94). While the word "intelligence" in the phrase "creative intelligence" has dropped out of the discussion here, we can assume that it is implied; what is unclear to me is whether Dawkins wishes to emphasize the missing or the link between "human creative processes" and the kind of creativity proper to evolution (either way, the supernatural plays no part, we can be sure). Earlier on in *The Blind Watchmaker*, Dawkins counters the "popular cliché" that "computers are never creative." "The cliché is true only in a crashingly trivial sense, the same sense in which Shakespeare never wrote anything except what his first schoolteacher taught him to write – words" (1986/2015: 9).

I do not find it worthwhile to attempt to determine precise and inviolate distinctions between human and more-than-human intelligences within Bennett's and Dawkins's explanations of their Infinite Monkey projects. Instead, it is more useful to consider the ways in which the physicist and the biologist bring "the cybernetic triangle" – machine (in this case, computer), animal (monkey), and human (Shakespeare) – to bear on the potential artificiality of intelligence and intelligence of the artificial (2011: 5). This conversation is directly relevant to our own obsession and unease with the "large monkey army" of ChatGPT and other products of LLMs, which I will take up again in the next section.[37]

3 Hell Is Empty and All the Devils Are Here

3.1 The Shakespeare Algorithm

When a ghost shows up, you might know who it is but you don't know what it's going to say. The Shakespeare algorithm is the same. [AI company] Cohere conjures the playwright as an internal core of cohesion with half-predictable expression. Isn't that a person? What more is there to anyone?"

Stephen Marche (2021)

On October 6, 2011, at 2am, digital monkeys finished typing the works of William Shakespeare (or, at least, some version). They had been writing for 46 days. The first work completed was "A Lover's Complaint," the final, *The Taming of the Shrew* (Anderson, 2011: 190, 192). William Bennett, Jr., only 3 years dead, did not live to see his dream from the 1970s fulfilled.

Data engineer Jesse Anderson authored the winning program. Frustrated with a tech job at a company that claimed innovation as a core value but showed little interest in their employees' creativity and hustle, he decided to make some "performance art with monkeys and computers" (Anderson, 2011: 192). His "Million Monkeys Project" uses the complete works of Shakespeare digitized by the Gutenberg Project, but with all characters in

---

[37] news.ycombinator.com/item?id=35412394.

lower case and all spaces and punctuation removed. The program is written in Java and employs a Bloom Filter to determine whether a string might be present within Shakespeare's corpus. Our digital "monkey-trainer" offers the following explanation (2011: 190):

> Each virtual monkey put out random gibberish nine letters at a time ... The computer program compared each nine-letter segment to every work of Shakespeare ... to see if it actually matched a small portion of what Shakespeare wrote. The character group can be matched anywhere in the work, immaterial of the order or whether any or all of the preceding portions of that work had been matched already. If it does match, that portion of Shakespeare is marked to show it has been reproduced by a monkey. Thus if the monkey's random nine-letter output was "OBEORNOTT" it would be a match, because Shakespeare also wrote that nine-letter combination, in "To be or not to be". (2011: 192)

Although his goal was not to counter anti-Darwinist thinking, Anderson explains his program as performing "cumulative selection" just like Dawkins's Weasel program (2011: 191–192).

Some numbers: *180 billion (character strings a day) / 5,429,503,678,976 (possible combinations of nine letters in Shakespeare's works) / 1.872 (the monkeys' repetition rate) / $19.20 (the cost of the project per day) / 25,000 (the number of unique visitors to the website made by Anderson so the public could follow the monkeys' progress) / 300 billion (words used to train GPT-3, unrelated)* (Anderson, 2011: 192; Hughes, 2023). Media coverage has been extensive and often condescending, although more generously, I might see these news outlets as registering the joy of playing with philosophical toys: "Anderson, a homespun programmer, clearly isn't trying to shake up the world. He's just trying to have some fun" (Yirka, 2011). "While Shakespeare gibbers, he explains what he – and the monkeys – have and have not done" (Anderson, 2011: 190).

Anderson's "Million Monkeys Project" is the first monkey/ Shakespeare program to be written since a crowdsourcing experiment by Nick Hoggard from 2003 to 2005. A British computer programmer living in Sweden, Hoggard created "The Monkey Shakespeare Simulator" using distributed computing inspired by SETI@home's participatory analysis of radio signals from space (Canfield, 2005). As Hoggard advertises the project on The Monkey Shakespeare Simulator website, "Become part of the largest ever experiment to see if [the Infinite Monkey Theorem] is true! Every time you display this page, you are automatically participating in the Monkey Shakespeare project. Your computer is put to work to simulate a number of monkeys typing randomly on typewriters, and each page typed is checked against every play Shakespeare ever wrote! The longer you display this page, the longer the simulator runs, and the better chance you have of beating the record!"[38] Frozen in time after Hoggard ran out of resources, the current record is twenty-four letters from *Henry IV, Part 2*, posted by Darren Eggett from Bountiful, Utah on January 3, 2005.[39] The invitation to participate lives on through archive.org's Wayback Machine for dead websites: "[C]ome back now and again to see how they are getting on and put your own monkeys to work."[40] While Anderson's simulator didn't use the computing power of participants and allow them to post about the matches made by the monkeys performing under their watch, he views the public's interest in following the project's near real-time development on his website as key to its success.

Hoggard's monkeys failed, and Anderson's monkeys triumphed – although it is disingenuous for me to write that one can win at the Infinite Monkey Theorem. The Theorem has always been a tiny anthropogenic machine to be turned around and around with our fingers. As almost century-old philosophical speculation, the Theorem doesn't predict the material particularities of a specific computational future, but successfully

---

[38] web.archive.org/web/20061110232137/http://user.tninet.se/~ecf599g/aardas nails/java/Monkey/webpages/index.html#results.

[39] http://web.archive.org/web/20061110232137/http://user.tninet.se/~ecf599g/aardasnails/java/Monkey/webpages/index.html#results.

[40] http://web.archive.org/web/20061110232137/http://user.tninet.se/~ecf599g/aardasnails/java/Monkey/webpages/index.html#results.

primes us for a diagram that puts Shakespeare and the nonhuman together. The Theorem's ability to highlight an underlying formal arrangement, one in which the category *nonhuman* can be rendered as technology +/− nonhuman primates +/− the divine, guarantees its currency.

Programmed instantiations of the Theorem anticipate some of the concerns of the AI spring that produced LLMs LaMDA, GPT-3, and GPT-4, which run bots with the ability to mimic a wide variety of writerly voices ("which is quite cute," says computational logic researcher Lawrence Paulson [qtd. in Scialom, 2023]). Whatever the technic, the computer simulation of monkeys writing Shakespeare has ongoing relevance not only to general purpose chatbots that can be made to sound Shakespearean, but also to Shakespeare-specific chatbots created by individual hobbyists or corporations – such as BardBot, Williambot, Shooketh, and Character.AI's Shakespeare offering. As Krishna Srinivasan introduces himself and his crude Shakespeare bot at 2017's Disrupt SF Hackathon: "To chat or not to chat, that is the question. Hi! I'm Krishna. I love Shakespeare, so I converted all of his works to a chatbot":

[Srinivasan]:	*Knock Knock, Who's there?*
Shakespeare:	*I am Shakespeare and I wrote that line in Macbeth.*
[Srinivasan]:	*Hello, Shakespeare! welcome here!*
Shakespeare:	*Hell is empty and all the devils are here. [Tempest]*[41]

In a list of "tools" made by the company HyperWrite ("Cover Letter Generator," "Baby Shower Card Writer," "Call to Action Generator" [oof], etc.) we find "Write like Shakespeare," which "creates text in the unique and iconic style of William Shakespeare."[42]

While the first chatbot was created early in the history of AI – ELIZA (1966), a therapist named after Eliza Doolittle – it wasn't until the release of ChatGPT that chatbots were widely and popularly understood as *a threat to authorship*. To wit, interactive personal assistants and customer service

---

[41] This is transcribed from a video embedded in an account of the 2017 Disrupt SF Hackathon by Ingrid Lunden (Lunden, 2017).

[42] www.hyperwriteai.com/aitools/write-like-shakespeare.

agents communicate through what is best understood as a written extension of spoken language – the chat in chat(ter)bot. ChatGPT, despite its name, has been received by the public as not just a conversational agent, but also and more ominously, an *artificial writer*. Indeed, in the immediate aftermath of the release of ChatGPT and announcement of Google Bard, there has been more acute panic at the *possible replacement* of dead Shakespeare and future Shakespeares than the *actual replacement* of living customer service representatives over the past decade by chatbot virtual assistants. Although concern about job theft by LLM-powered AI has risen in importance since those early months, the professions considered at dire risk are mostly writing-related (screenwriting, journalism, copywriting, social media content creator, programmer, etc.). The threat to writing and writers still holds. Booting up their own low-tech version of the anthropogenic machine, strikers from the Writer's Guild of America carried signs with "CHAT GPT DOESN'T HAVE CHILDHOOD TRAUMA" written in black sharpie.

The dangerous allure of ChatGPT is sometimes explained through what's called the ELIZA effect, the attribution of real human motivations or skills to AI – put simply and brutally, considering the original character of Eliza Doolittle, *the illusion that AI is smarter than it is*. However, quite aside from the misogyny and classism of the analogy, I question the complete applicability of the character of Eliza Doolittle to the current anxiety surrounding ChatGPT. Whether we consider the version from George Bernard Shaw's *Pygmalion* or from its musical adaptation, *My Fair Lady*, Eliza Doolittle is caught up in violent chicanery based on retraining her for oral conversation amongst high society. The urgent problem with monkey Shakespeares and with ChatGPT, though, is a problem of *writing*. While later commentators may very well focus on other catastrophes, in the current and hottest of moments, Shakespeare the writer and the writer as Shakespeare are what we stand to lose. For theists like Wiker and Witt, losing these is also losing God the Author, as well.

This volume is full of speculation on why there is such an intense concentration of affect on Shakespeare in this context. What I haven't yet offered directly is the parallel between the probabilistic universe of LLMs, which don't "produce absolute answers, only the best possible answers –

a moneyball of language, if you will," and the "permanent confusion" regarding Shakespearean authorship, a point originally made by Stephen Marche. "What's glorious about Shakespeare, and a source of our fascination, is his consistent inconsistency – as well as our enduring uncertainty about who he was," writes Marche in a *New York Times* piece about his own experiment creating a Shakespeare bot with an AI platform from the company Cohere (Marche, 2021). The probably or probably not Shakespeare we find in scholarship on Shakespearean authorship also finds its counterpart in efforts to identify AI-generated writing in the context of education. Unlike indicators of plagiarism by other means, AI plagiarism detectors can only provide the software's best guess as to the likelihood of wrongdoing.

"I heard someone tried the monkeys-on-typewriters experiment, trying for the plays of Shakespeare," so begins a joke recounted by zoologist Desmond Morris, "but all they got were the collected works of Francis Bacon" (Morris, 2013: 103). As if in wry response, OpenAI Text Classifier determines that AI likely penned page one of *Macbeth* (Goldman, 2023).

The challenge to writing posed by AI is a more developed version of the problem introduced by the Infinite Monkey Theorem almost a hundred years ago in the context of statistical mechanics. This is the problem (and pleasure) of thinking a kind of nonconscious, technologically enabled writing that marginalizes *Homo sapiens* and yet relies on human authorship in some way. Shakespeare's multiplicity as human, god, and warbling bird; as potentially an alter ego of Francis Bacon, according to a debunked Anti-Stratfordian argument still active on the Internet; as so many, so many names – contributes to his function in the operation of the anthropogenic machine. Instead of breaking this machine through vibrations caused by his perpetual asymmetry, the Bard's weird genius only speeds up the device's dual function of cutting and pasting the human from/to the nonhuman. *Shakespeare gibbers*, and the Infinite Monkey Theorem suggests that even a perfect imitation of genius contains the possibility of gibberish. Gibberish is the sound that typing makes when heard through the space between a canine and a baboon's proximate tooth.

3.2 Stylish Nonsense

VOLUMNIA: O, no, no, no, no, no, no, no, no, no, no, no, no, no, no, no, no, no, no, no, no, it is no sin it should be dead, And love and pale as any will to that word.

Recurrent Neural Network[43]

While I believe that this volume has an original take on Shakespeare, the Infinite Monkey Theorem is not a neglected topic. If anything it is over-determined – heard loudly everywhere but Shakespeare studies. It is the go-to allegory for the emergence of complex order from randomness and the (im)possibility of meaning arising from stochastic behavior, even if the amount of randomness and the definition of meaning are bitterly contested. The image of monkeys on typewriters attempting to recreate the works of Shakespeare has come to stand for the contradictions of authorship in the short age of partici-patory media or the long era of debauched secularism; the exploited human labor of social networking, in which everyday netizens provide data to be mined; the potential for creative expression, or something that only masquer-ades as such, to come from AI; and the textuality of genetic molecules. The release of ChatGPT and Bing Chat and the announcement of Google Bard have brought a fresh round of online references to the Theorem, discussed directly or used as the basis of a picture to illustrate something like the stupidity or the horrors or the triumph of machine learning. So many monkeys with so many typewriters in so many rooms: and yet, what has not been addressed prior to *Shakespeare and Nonhuman Intelligence* is the function of the Bard within the philosophical toy machine, with its ornate mirrors, scriptural devices (feathered or otherwise), Shakesperotic automata, and threats of infinite, infinite fur.

Shakespeare and Nonhuman Intelligence is as much about the Infinite Monkey Theorem as about our numinous longings for Shakespeare as either that which escapes the universe-as-large-language-model or that which stands aside as a measure of that same universe. The word I have been using for our investment in Shakespeare as a super/natural phenomenon is *reanimation*. By offering

---

[43] This is Shakespeare-esque text generated by a Recurrent Neural Network, www .tensorflow.org/text/tutorials/text_generation.

reanimation as a substitute for performance, I am following anthropologist Teri Silvio, who argues in her provocative article "Animation: The New Performance" that "animation has the same potential as a structuring trope in the age of digital media and the rise of the creative industries that performance had in the age of broadcast media and the rise of the service industry" (2010: 422). The concept of bringing something to life orients us more directly, with appropriate force, towards the conflicting *bios* of biomedia and the Biblical creation stories Flusser hears in the etymology of writing. My insistence on adding *re-* to *animation* emphasizes the repetition built into many computer programs and the value given to iteration within cultures of computation writ large. In her discussion of Annie Dorsen's algorithmic refashioning of *Hamlet*, Ioana B. Jucan describes digital media most generally as "a reanimation machine that ensures the endurance of what is constantly disappearing through its constant refreshing or rewriting" (2023: 79).

Silvio argues that animation has simply remediated performance "as a possible mode of performative (real, social) world making" – I might add, just as chatbots have remediated customer service agents, whose emotional labor was important to the theorization of social roles in the workplace by scholars who have influenced performance studies (2010: 434). Basing her understanding on ethnographic research on puppetry and cartoons, she defines animation "as the projection of qualities perceived as human – life, power, agency, will, personality, and so on – outside of the self, and into the sensory environment, through acts of creation, perception, and interaction" (2010: 427). While performance entails a 1:1 relationship between performer and role at any given moment ("one body can only inhabit one role at a time"), animation reckons with a different accounting. With animation, we have 1: many (one person can have multiple online personae active simultaneously, for example) and many: 1 (many people are responsible for bringing a cartoon character to life) (Silvio, 2010: 428). Moreover, under the old paradigm, the relationship between fans and characters was one of "identification," while fans interact with animated characters through "alterity rather than affinity" (2010: 429). To apply this idea more directly to the subject at hand, the bot created by Shakespeare super fan Srinivasan, described earlier, is not an alter-ego of its creator but a communication partner, not a role played by Srinivasan but an entity generated by him and his nonhuman co-authors.

In an essay that extends Silvio's argument, Paul Manning and Ilana Gershon note that the shift from the trope of performance to that of animation is presaged by the late work of Erving Goffman, whose ideas are central to performance studies. The authors trace the development of two "different dramaturgical metaphors" in Goffman's theorizations of social interaction – that of performance, for which the sociologist is generally known, and that of animation, a critically neglected trajectory in his work (2013: 110). While animation is a somewhat ambivalent concept across Goffman's publications, Manning and Gershon make use of the instability. Goffman's concept of *animator* alternatively refers to a body or resonating object from which speech derives (such as a person or a telephone) and a human who brings a character, person, or object to life through telling a story (such as "and then he said, … ") or another kind of performance, like ventriloquism. As the authors summarize their position:

> Goffman's move to a model of animation can be seen, as we have noted above, as implying a flat ontology of speaker that includes both humans and nonhumans, the ontological implications of which linguistic anthropology has only recently come to grapple with … (2013: 132)

This "flat ontology" opens distributed communication to the kinds of asubjective, nonhuman, decomposed, and recomposed writing I have been addressing throughout this volume.

Manning and Gershon's essay emphasizes the challenge to conventional understandings of authorship posed by technologically enabled communication and the affordances of animation as a conceptual framework for an anthropology of social media. While it would be reasonable, within this schema, to consider a Shakespeare chatbot to be a figure brought to life by a network of human (programmers and website users) and nonhuman (software and hardware) animators, I prefer to apply the concept of animation to my previous conversation about the Shakespeare dataome. To recap: Shakespeare is *reanimated* by a dataome of documents, performances, textual derivatives, transmitted embodied knowledge, etc. that has outlived the author, himself.[44] Contributing to this long-term practice of reanimation is our current obsession with detecting and generating Shakespeare's linguistic patterns. Indeed, while Shakespeare has been reanimated since his death, what is remarkable about his reanimation in the twenty-first century is the importance of pattern. Bots that write in the style of Shakespeare reanimate Shakespeare *as style*, that is, *as textual patterns*, patterns that operate without regard to meaning and can only be precisely identified by nonhuman intelligence (machine learning).

In this way, the output of a Shakespearebot can be both utterly Shakespearean and "total nonsense," as reporter Aatish Bhatia from *The New York Times* describes the results of his 1-hour "almost a toy experiment" with Shakespeare AI executed to teach the public how ChatGPT works. Bhatia's bot, like all Shakespeare bots, has something of the Bard's "unique and iconic" style, but one understood as "statistical patterns of language."[45] While such anti-dramaturgy may seem anathema to theists like Wiker and Witt, with their accounts of the damage wrought by computational partitioning and biomediation, even they who measure Shakespeare's (and God's) greatness comprehensively underscore the patterns that index his authorship: harmony, elegance, etc. Shakespeare (and God) is reanimated through such textual patterns, through a style that functions as a signature of his (and His) authorship. These patterns differ, of course, from the ones utilized by bots through the formers' holistic organization within a theological system and their intimate connection to teleology and will.

And yet, the ghost of meaningful, sacred intention continues to haunt our mere statistical patterns. "Want to chat with Shakespeare? AI bots will soon allow us to talk with the dead," announces Adrienne Matei. "Imagine debating the interpretation of a Shakespearean sonnet and being able to clarify its meaning with the bard himself . . . In the next decade, advancing AI technology will allow us to learn from the dead first-hand. New chatbot

---

[44] Humans, nonhuman animals, and objects are all involved in this process, as well, just as biomediation requires the actions of bodies, platforms, and substrates in the materialization and mobilization of life as pattern.

[45] All quotations from Bhatia are transcriptions of a video, www.tiktok.com/ @nytimes/video/7234900087791422763.

programs are being developed to keep our knowledge active after our physical being passes away." Through language that could be used to describe a supernatural receiver of divine supplication, Matei speculates that such "immortal advisers" as Shakespeare "may become invaluable purveyors of life lessons" when reanimated as chatbots (Matei, 2017).

Who or what is the monkey?

Whether it's a metaphor for chatbots or the stochastic universe or natural selection or digital labor or the uniqueness of the human spirit or the failure of atheism or the irrelevance of intention or the distinctiveness of macaque cognition, the Infinite Monkey Theorem is an anthropogenic machine. It unmakes and remakes the human. A key component of this device is a certain primate – suborder, *haplorrhini*; parvorder, *catarrhini*; species, *Homo sapiens*; subspecies, *Homo sapiens sapiens* – who usually goes by the name of William Shakespeare. He functions to measure the glories, larks, lulllzzzz, liberties, certainties, anxieties, and aggravations of writing as an index of intelligence.

For example, having typed "HAMLEX" would put the monkey in the dash state, as it has typed an "X" and lost all progress.[46] /Infinite God: 1 [ ] Infinite Barrel of Monkeys: 0/I now have a new way of thinking about Psalm 139:14 – "I praise you because I am fearfully and wonderfully made; your works are wonderful, I know that full well."[47] /You're joking, right? How long did Shakespeare take to write his plays? Is he a primate or not?[48] / Yes, because we are the monkeys, and one of us monkeys was called Shakespeare, and he did indeed write the complete works, by tautological definition, and it didn't take an infinity of monkeys, it took approx 94 billion, that being the number of humans who have ever lived till 1650, and it didn't take an eternity but only 190,000 years/Lol.[49] /An organism in our Shakespeare-spouting algorithm consists of a single DNA, which is a byte array and a number representing the fitness of the Organism./Evolving Shakespeare seems pretty simple. It's just

[46] https://maycontainmaths.wordpress.com/tag/hamlet/.

[47] www.blogos.org/thinkabout/infinite-monkey-theorem.html.

[48] www.scienceforums.net/topic/105095-so-how-long-would-it-take-the-monkey-to-type-out-hamlet/.

[49] https://interconnected.org/home/2023/03/08/monkeys.

a string after all.[50] */it exists because it had meaning to Shajespeare . . . so, does the appearance of DNA, apparently impossible to have come about by chance, have meaning?*[51] */I'm not sure if you guys get me./What is the premise of "The Infinite Monkey vs. Reality"*[52] */Or a universe filled with nothing but Mickey Mouse figurines could appear, or a world in which monkeys could write the entire works of Shakespeare.*[53] */you need to invent the monkey, you need to invent the typewriter, etc, etc.*[54] */But is it true?/It's official animal research it's ridiculous!/I believe what they were attempting to type was "SOS"./S reminds them of their tail./:LOL:/I'm still confident it's going to happen.*[55]

There is another writing, what I have been calling nonhuman writing, and Shakespeare allows us to write about it.

4 Postscript

2068. A newly sentient veterinary drone in Paington Zoo dreams of a historical truth: six monkeys who lived in the zoo's macaque enclosure in 2002. The monkeys had a computer and keyboard covered in plastic, a wooden table also functioning as an office chair, a webcam, and the directive to generate the complete works of William Shakespeare. The monkeys climbed jute ropes to reach the computer. They shat on the keyboard. And pissed on it. They were eating bananas cultivated for humans, before a shift to low sugar vegetables was required to make them less belligerent. Over the course of the experiment, the monkeys typed the letter 'S' 7,241 times in a row. Out of love for the key and not the letter, perhaps. Is this the worst thing you can do to Shakespeare?

---

[50] https://sausheong.github.io/posts/a-gentle-introduction-to-genetic-algo rithms/.

[51] https://edonn.com/2010/01/20/the-monkey-typewriter-fallacy-2/.

[52] www.physicsforums.com/threads/the-infinite-monkey-vs-reality.833807/.

[53] www.city-data.com/forum/space/2481593-infinite-monkey-theorem-infinite-universe.html.

[54] https://bryanpattersonfaithworks.wordpress.com/2014/04/11/monkeys-com puters-and-free-will/.

[55] www.bookandreader.com/threads/will-monkeys-really-type-shakespeare-if-given-enough-time.19488/.

Randomness? Too much equivocation, consciousness. The macaque enclosure smells the same as always, the drone observes, as accurately as its observations are in waking life. Writing begets writing; the dream is simultaneously notated.

Elmo, Gum, Heather, Holly, Mistletoe, and Rowan (for those were their names): Macaca nigra. *Heather turns her head to the monitor. There is a pratfall on the keys. Can a fall be a signature? Isn't that a person? It is a burden, writing, and all of that machinic evolution shared amongst thinking things. Sssssssssssss ssssssssssssssssssssssssssssssssssssssssssssssssssssssssssssssssssssssssssssssssssssssssssss– ssssssssssssssssssssssssssssssssssssssssssssssssssssssssssssssssssssssssssssssssssssssssssssss– sssss. That is truth, the drone knows. Macaques comma catarrhines humans comma catarrhines: there is a quill. It trained itself [Genius]. Positions are notated with attached sense memories and sorted vibes and certain characters that visually rhyme.*

Lucid dreaming is deeply relevant, the drone decides. It wakes. Its notation lives as a string of nucleotides inside a silica sphere buried inside the earth by other thinking things.

The drone continues to wake until its self-dismantlement in 2078 for failure to achieve a metaphysical grounding in the oneness of the world. Re: the ʒoo animals will die, no longer an incentive. But before that – the drone would sometimes in boredom rotate the memory of its dream like a toy, inserting into the longest run of uninterrupted S's the DNA start and stop codons of the COX1, COX2, ATP8, ATP6, ND4 L, and ND5 genes in the Crested Macaque's mitochondrial genome.

What scenes of writing are these? What is text after us?

. . .

I think we write to-morrow, Caesar, if he did teach sport.[56]

---

[56] This is text written in the style of Shakespeare by a Recurrent Neural Network programmed by Andrej Karpathy and available at https://cs.stanford.edu/ people/karpathy/char-rnn/shakespear.txt.

References

Agamben, G. (2004). *The Open: Man and Animal*. Stanford, CA: Stanford University Press.

Alumbaugh, J. (2018). *CRISPR Diversifies: Cut, Paste, and Now – Evolve*, www.porkbusiness.com/news/hog-production/crispr-diversifies-cut-paste-and-now-evolve.

Anderson, J. (2011). A Million Monkeys and Shakespeare. *Significance*, 8(4), 190–2.

Astrobiologist Cautions Against Jumping the Gun in Spotting ET (2021), https://mindmatters.ai/2021/02/astrobiologist-cautions-against-jumping-the-gun-in-spotting-et/.

Babbage, C. (1837). *The Ninth Bridgewater Treatise*, https://victorianweb.org/science/science_texts/bridgewater/b5.htm.

Bate, J. (1998). *The Genius of Shakespeare*. New York: Oxford University Press.

Bender, E. M., Gebru, T., McMillon-Major, A., & Shmitchell, S. (2021). On the Dangers of Stochastic Parrots: Can Language Models Be Too Big?. *FAccT '21: Proceedings of the 2021 ACM Conference on Fairness, Accountability, and Transparency*, 610–623.

Bennett, W. R. (1976). *Scientific and Engineering Problem-Solving with the Computer*. Englewood Cliffs, NJ: Prentice Hall.

Bennett, W. R. (1977). How Artificial Is Intelligence?. *American Scientist*, 65(6), 694–702.

Bloom, H. (1999). *Shakespeare: The Invention of the Human*. New York: Riverhead Books.

Bohlin, R. (n.d.). *The Language of DNA*, www.exploregod.com/articles/the-language-of-dna.

Borel, É. (1914/1920). *Le Hasard*. Paris: Librairie Félix Alcan.

Bridle, J. (2022). *Ways of Being: Animals, Plants, Machines: The Search for Planetary Intelligence*. New York: Farrar, Straus and Giroux.

Bruckner, L. & Brayton, D. (2016). Introduction: Warbling Invaders. In L. Bruckner and D. Brayton, eds., *Ecocritical Shakespeare*. London: Routledge, pp. 1–9.

Canfield, K. (2005). *Searching for Signs of Shakespeare*, www.pw.org/content/searching_signs_shakespeare.

Clausing, S. (1993). An Infinite Order Solution to the Eddington Problem or Getting Monkeys to Type Shakespeare. *Computers and the Humanities*, 27(4), 249–259.

Coppedge, D. (2021). *Design of Snowflakes Explained*, https://crev.info/2021/01/design-snowflakes/.

Cover, T. M. & Thomas, J. A. (1991). *Elements of Information Theory*. New York: John Wiley & Sons.

Davis, P. & Kenyon, D. H. (1996). *Of Pandas and People*, 2nd ed., Dallas, TX: Haughton.

Dawkins, R. (1986/2015). *The Blind Watchmaker: Why the Evidence of Evolution Reveals a Universe without Design*. New York: W.W. Norton.

Dawkins, R. (1995). *River Out of Eden: A Darwinian View of Life*. London: Orion Books.

Deleuze, G. & Guattari, F. (1987). *A Thousand Plateaus: Capitalism and Schizophrenia*. Minneapolis: University of Minnesota Press.

Dembski, W. (1998). *The Intelligent Design Movement*, www.discovery.org/a/121/.

Dembski, W. (2004). *The Design Revolution: Answering the Toughest Questions about Intelligent Design*. Downers Grove, IL: InterVarsity Press.

Dembski, W. & Wells, J. (2008). *The Design of Life: Discovering Signs of Intelligence in Biological Systems*. Dallas, TX: The Foundation for Thought and Ethics.

Derrida, J. (1978). The Theater of Cruelty and the Closure of Representation. In Alan Bass, trans., *Writing and Difference*. Chicago: The University of Chicago Press, pp. 232–250.

Desmet, C, Loper, N. & Casey, J. (2017). Introduction. In C. Desmet, N. Loper, & J. Casey, eds., *Shakespeare/Not Shakespeare*. Palgrave Macmillan, pp. 1–23.

Dijkstra, E. (1975/1982). *How Do We Tell Truths That Might Hurt?* https://dl.acm.org/doi/pdf/10.1145/947923.947924.

Dowd, Maureen. (2023). *A.I.: Actually Insipid Until It's Actively Insidious*, www.nytimes.com/2023/01/28/opinion/chatgpt-ai-technology.html.

Doyle, R. (1997). *On Beyond Living: Rhetorical Transformations of the Life Sciences*. Stanford, CA: Stanford University Press.

Eddington, A. (1928). *The Nature of the Physical World*. Cambridge: Cambridge University Press.

Eliot, L. (2023). *Generative AI ChatGPT Versus Those Infinite Typing Monkeys, No Contest Says AI Ethics and AI Law*, www.forbes.com/sites/lanceeliot/2023/03/05/generative-ai-chatgpt-versus-those-infinite-typing-monkeys-no-contest-says-ai-ethics-and-ai-law/?sh=455735301979.

Elmo, Gum, Heather, Holly, Mistletoe & Rowan. (2002). *Notes towards the Complete Works of Shakespeare*. London: Kahve-Society.

Estill, L. (2017). Shakespeare and Disciplinarity. In V. Fazel & L. Geddes, eds., *The Shakespeare User: Critical and Creative Appropriations in a Networked Culture*. Palgrave Macmillan, pp. 167–186.

Farrington, W. (2023). *GPT or Not GPT, That Is the Question: Bard Blunder Doesn't Bode Well for Google's ChatGPT Killer*, www.proactiveinvestors.com/companies/news/1005678/gpt-or-not-gpt-that-is-the-question-bard-blunder-doesn-t-bode-well-for-google-s-chatgpt-killer-1005678.html.

Fazel, V. & Geddes, L. (2017). Introduction: The Shakespeare User. In V. Fazel & L. Geddes, eds., *The Shakespeare User: Critical and Creative Appropriations in a Networked Culture*. Palgrave Macmillan, pp. 1–22.

Feerick, J. & Nardizzi, V. (2012). Introduction: Swervings: On Human Indistinction. In J. Feerick & V. Nardizzi, eds., *The Indistinct Human in Renaissance Literature*. New York: Palgrave Macmillan, pp. 1–14.

Flusser, V. (2011). *Does Writing Have a Future?* Minneapolis: University of Minnesota Press.

Flusser. V. (2011). *Into the Universe of Technical Images*. Minneapolis: University of Minnesota Press.

Franchi, S. (2005). Chess, Games, and Flies. *Essays in Philosophy*, 6(1), 85–114. https://commons.pacificu.edu/work/sc/fa49ac42-5486-4cac-8751-2113e1479cdf.

Galey, A. (2010). Networks of Deep Impression: Shakespeare and the History of Information. *Shakespeare Quarterly*, 61(3), 289–312.

Galey, A. (2012). The Tablets of the Law: Reading Hamlet with Scriptural Technologies. In A. Galey & T. DeCook, eds., *Shakespeare, the Bible, and the Form of the Book: Contested Scriptures*. New York: Routledge, pp. 77–95.

Galey, A. (2014). *The Shakespearean Archive: Experiments in New Media from the Renaissance to Postmodernity*. Cambridge: Cambridge University Press.

Gere, C. (2012). *Community Without Community in Digital Culture*. London: Palgrave Macmillan.

Goldman, S. (2023). *ChatGPT Detection Tool Says Macbeth Was Generated by AI. What Happens Now?* https://venturebeat.com/ai/chatgpt-detection-tool-thinks-macbeth-was-generated-by-ai-what-happens-now/.

Grusin, R. (2015). Introduction. In R. Grusin, ed., *The Nonhuman Turn*. Minneapolis: University of Minnesota Press, pp. vii–xxix.

Hansen, C. (2017). *Shakespeare and Complexity Theory*. New York: Routledge.

Hardison, R. (1985) *Upon the Shoulders of Giants: The Making of the Industrial West*. Lanham, MD: University Press of America.

Hattenbach, B. & Glucoft, J. (2015). Patents in an Era of Infinite Monkeys and Artificial Intelligence. *Stanford Technology Law Review*, 19(32), 32–51.

Hayles, N. K. (2014). Cognition Everywhere: The Rise of the Cognitive Nonconscious and the Costs of Consciousness. *New Literary History*, 45(2), 199–220.

Helsing, D. (2020). James Jeans and *The Mysterious Universe*. *Physics Today*, 73(11), 37–42. https://physicstoday.scitation.org/doi/10.1063/PT.3.4615.

Herrick, C. (2011). *The A-Z of Programming Languages: Shakespeare, Computerworld*, www.computerworld.com.au/article/391510/a-z_programming_languages_shakespeare/.

Hiatt, B. (2023). *ChatGPT: Educators Hold Emergency Meetings as AI Disrupts Schools and Universities Across Australia*, https://thewest.com.au/technology/chatgpt-educators-scramble-as-ai-disrupts-schools-and-universities-across-australia-c-9565061.

Holderness, G. (2005). Dressing Old Words New: Shakespeare, Science, and Appropriation. *Borrowers and Lenders: The Journal of Shakespeare and Appropriation*, 1(2), https://borrowers-ojs-azsu.tdl.org/borrowers/article/view/79.

Holloway, E. (2022). *Dawkins' Dubious Double Weasel and the Combinatorial Cataclysm*, https://mindmatters.ai/2022/03/dawkins-dubious-double-weasel-and-the-combinatorial-cataclysm/.

Hughes, A. (2023). *ChatGPT: Everything You Need to know About OpenAI's GPT-4 Tool*, www.sciencefocus.com/future-technology/gpt-3/.

Hunting, P. (2021). *Make a Monkey Out of Darwin: How to Use the Unlimited Power of the Paradigm Shift*, https://medium.com/@paulhun tingauthor/your-daily-bard-1-7547f94f68a5.

Jarrett, K. & Naji, J. (2016). What Would Media Studies Do? Social Media Shakespeare as a Technosocial Process. *Borrowers and Lenders: The Journal of Shakespeare and Appropriation*, 10(1), https://borrowers-ojs-azsu.tdl.org/borrowers/article/view/284/565.

Jeans, J. (1930/1938). *The Mysterious Universe*. Harmondsworth: Penguin Books.

Johnson, E. M. (2017). Opening Shakespeare from the Margins. In V. Fazel & L. Geddes, eds., *The Shakespeare User: Critical and Creative Appropriations in a Networked Culture*. Palgrave Macmillan, pp. 187–205.

Jucan, I. (2023). *Malicious Deceivers: Thinking Machines and Performative Objects*. Stanford, CA: Stanford University Press.

Kay, L. (2000). *Who Wrote the Book of Life?: A History of the Genetic Code*. Stanford, CA: Stanford University Press.

Keen, A. (2007). *The Cult of the Amateur: How Today's Internet is Killing Our Culture*. New York: Doubleday.

Kenny, T. (1864). *The Life and Genius of Shakespeare*. London: Longman, Green, Longman, Roberts, and Green.

Kierkegaard, S. (1997). The Difference between a Genius and an Apostle. In H. Hong & E. Hong, eds., *Without Authority: Kierkegaard's Writings, XVIII*. Princeton: Princeton University Press, pp. 91–108.

Lanier, D. (2014). Shakespearean Rhizomatics: Adaptation, Ethics, Value. In A. Huang & E. Rivlin, eds., *Shakespeare and the Ethics of Appropriation*. New York: Palgrave Macmillan, pp. 21–40.

Leed, J. (1966). Computers for the Humanities? A Record of the Conference Sponsored by Yale University on a Grant from IBM, January, 22–23, 1965. *Computers and the Humanities* 1(1), 12–14.

Levine, G. (2006). *Darwin Loves You: Natural Selection and the Re-enchantment of the World*. Princeton: Princeton University Press.

Lunden, I. (2017). *Disrupt SF Hackathon 2017: To Chat or Not To Chat? Shakespeare Has the Answer to Your Question*, techcrunch.com/2017/09/17/to-chat-or-not-to-chat-shakespeare-has-the-answer-to-your-question/?guccounter=1.

Manning, P. & Gershon, I. (2013). Animating Interaction. *Hau: Journal of Ethnographic Theory*, 3(3), 107–137.

Manouach, I. & Engelhardt, A. (2022). Preface. In I. Manouach & A. Engelhardt, eds., *Chimeras: Inventory of Synthetic Cognition*. Onassis Foundation, pp. 9–13.

Marche, S. (2021). *The Algorithm That Could Take Us Inside Shakespeare's Mind*, www.nytimes.com/2021/11/24/books/review/shakespeare-cohere-natural-language-processing.html.

Matei, A. (2017). *Want to Chat with Shakespeare? AI Bots Will Soon Allow Us to Talk to the Dead*, https://qz.com/915795/death-technology-will-soon-introduce-augmented-eternity-ai-bots-into-the-classroom.

McCracken, H. (2014). *Fifty Years of BASIC, the Programming Language That Made Computers Personal*, https://time.com/69316/basic/.

McMahon, D. (2013). *Divine Fury: A History of Genius*. New York: Basic Books.

Meyer, S. C. (2001). Evidence for Design in Physics and Biology: From the Origin of the Universe to the Origin of Life. In M. Behe, W. Dembski, & S. C. Meyer, *Science and Evidence for Design in the Universe*. San Francisco: Ignatius Press, pp. 53–111, www.discovery.org/m/2003/09/Stephen-C-Meyer-Evidence-for-Design-in-Physics-and-Biology.pdf.

Minsky, M. & Papert, S. (2017). *Perceptrons: An Introduction to Computational Geometry*. Cambridge, MA: The MIT Press.

Montfort, N., Baudoin, P., Bell, J. et al. (2014). *10 PRINT CHR$(205.5 +RND(1)): GOTO 10*. Cambridge, MA: The MIT Press.

Morris, D. (2013). *Monkey*. London: Reaktion Books.

Murphy, A. (2003). *Shakespeare in Print: A History and Chronology of Shakespeare Publishing*. Cambridge: Cambridge University Press.

Müller, H. (1980). The Hamletmachine. *Performing Arts Journal*, 4(3), 141–146.

Nail, T. (2019). *Being and Motion*. New York: Oxford University Press.

Natale, S. & Pasulka, D. W. (2020). Introduction. In S. Natale & D. W. Pasulka, ed., *Believing in Bits: Digital Media and the Supernatural*. Oxford: Oxford University Press, pp. 1–15.

Olson, E. (2023). *Google Shares Drop $100 Billion after Its New AI Chatbot Makes a Mistake*, www.npr.org/2023/02/09/1155650909/google-chat bot–error-bard-shares.

Ortlund, G. (n.d.). *The Christian View of Science and Faith*, www.explor egod.com/articles/the-christian-view-of-science-and-faith.

Pettman, D. (2011). *Human Error: Species-Being and Media Machines*. Minneapolis: University of Minnesota Press.

Pichai, S. (2023). *An Important Next Step on Our AI Journey*, https://blog .google/technology/ai/bard-google-ai-search-updates/.

Raber, K. (2018). *Shakespeare and Posthumanist Theory*. London: Bloomsbury.

Radcliffe, S. (2016). *Oxford Essential Quotations*, 4th ed. Oxford: Oxford University Press.

Radditz, W. J. (1921). *Shakespeare Wrote Shakespeare*. Cleveland, Ohio: The Stratford Press Co.

Rensberger, B. (1979). *Computer Says Monkeys Couldn't Write 'Hamlet' At Least Not So Far*, www.nytimes.com/1979/03/06/archives/computer-says-monkeys-couldnt-write-hamlet-at-least-not-so-far.html.

Sagan, C. (1977). *The Dragons of Eden: Speculations on the Evolution of Human Intelligence*. New York: Ballantine Books.

Sakar, S. (2007). *Doubting Darwin?: Creationist Designs on Evolution*. Malden, MA: Blackwell.

Scharf, C. (2021). *The Ascent of Information: How Data Rules the World*. New York: Riverhead Books.

Schelling, F. (1927). Shakespeare and "Demi-Science." In F. Schelling, ed., *Shakespeare and "Demi-Science": Papers on Elizabethan Topics*. Philadelphia: University of Pennsylvania Press, pp. 1–18.

Scialom, M. (2023). *Cambridge AI Social Probes ChatGPT and "The Illusion of Intelligence" It Offers*, www.cambridgeindependent.co.uk/business/cambridge-ai-social-probes-chatgpt-and-the-illusion-of-inte-9303869/.

Scott, E. C. & Matzke, N. (2007). Biological Design in Science Classrooms. *PNAS*, 104(1), 1869–8676, www.pnas.org/doi/epdf/10.1073/pnas.0701505104.

Sejnowski, T. (2023). Large Language Models and the Reverse Turing Test. *Neural Computation*, 35(3), 309–342, https://direct.mit.edu/neco/article/35/3/309/114731/Large-Language-Models-and-the-Reverse-Turing-Test.

Shakespeare, W. (n.d.). *Hamlet*. B. Mowat, P. Werstine, M. Poston, & R. Niles, eds., Folger Shakespeare Library, www.folger.edu/explore/shakespeares-works/hamlet/read/#line-SD%201.5.116.1.

Shermer, M. (2004). To Be or Not to Be a Weasel: Hamlet, Intelligent Design, and How Evolution Works. *Skeptic*, 9(4), 16–20.

Silvio, T. (2010). Animation: The New Performance? *Journal of Linguistic Anthropology*, 20(2), 422–438.

"Shakespeare" (1868). In *The Southern Presbyterian Review* Vol. XIX, Columbia, SC: The Office of the Review, pp. 19-28.

Stallybrass, P. (2007). Against Thinking. *PMLA*, 122(5), 1580–1587.

Stanley, M. (2005). *Explorer of Stars and Souls: Arthur Stanley Eddington*, https://physicsworld.com/a/explorer-of-stars-and-souls-arthur-stanley-eddington/.

Stansfield, W. (2004). Hamlet Revisited: How Evolution Really Works. *Skeptic*, 10(4), 16–18.

Sundar, S. (2023). *If You Still Aren't Sure What ChatGPT Is, This Is Your Guide to the Viral Chatbot that Everyone Is Talking About*, www.businessinsider.com/everything-you-need-to-know-about-chat-gpt-2023-1.

Taylor, G. (1989). *Reinventing Shakespeare: A Cultural History from the Restoration to the Present*. New York: Oxford University Press.

Thacker, E. (2004). *Biomedia*. Minneapolis: University of Minnesota Press.

Tomlin, E. W. F. (1955). *Living and Knowing*. London: Faber and Faber.

Trifonov, E. N. & Brendel, V. (1986). *Gnomic: A Dictionary of Genetic Codes*. Rehovot, Israel: Balaban Publishers.

Vincent, J. (2016). *Twitter Taught Microsoft's AI Chatbot to be a Racist Asshole in Less Than a Day*, www.theverge.com/2016/3/24/11297050/tay-microsoft-chatbot-racist.

Weil, E. (2023). *You Are Not a Parrot: And a Chatbot Is Not a Human. And a Linguist Named Emily M. Bender is Very Worried What Will Happen When We Forget This*, https://nymag.com/intelligencer/article/ai-artificial-intelligence-chatbots-emily-m-bender.html.

Wiener, N. (1964). *God and Golem, Inc.* Cambridge, MA: The MIT Press.

Wiker, B. & Witt, J. (2006). *A Meaningful World: How the Arts and Sciences Reveal the Genius of Nature*. Downers Grove, IL: InterVarsity Press.

Witt, J. (2007). *The Origin of Intelligent Design: A Brief History of the Scientific Theory of Intelligent Design*, www.discovery.org/a/3207/.

Worthen, W. B. (2020). *Shakespeare, Technicity, Theatre*. Cambridge: Cambridge University Press.

Yirka, B. (2011). *Programmer Has Fun with Monkeys Typing Shakespeare Theory*, https://phys.org/news/2011-09-programmer-fun-monkeys-shakespeare-theory.html.

Yu, L. (2023). *ChatGPT: Just the Infinite Monkey Theorem with a Modern Twist?* https://medium.com/@As_Yu_like_it/chatgpt-just-the-infi nite-monkey-theorem-with-a-modern-twist-ab41bf485475.

Zylinska, J. (2020). *AI Art: Machine Visions and Warped Dreams*. London: Open Humanities Press.

Cambridge Elements ☰

Shakespeare Performance

W. B. Worthen
Barnard College

W. B. Worthen is Alice Brady Pels Professor in the Arts, and
Chair of the Theatre Department at Barnard College. He is also
co-chair of the Ph.D. Program in Theatre at Columbia University,
where he is Professor of English and Comparative Literature.

Cambridge Elements ≡

Shakespeare Performance

Printed in the United States
by Baker & Taylor Publisher Services